FIFTY KEY WORDS: COMPARATIVE RELIGION

Other Titles in the Series

Fifty Key Words: Theology, by F. G. Healey

Fifty Key Words: Philosophy, by Keith Ward

Fifty Key Words: The Church, by William Stewart

Fifty Key Words: Sociology, edited by David Martin

Fifty Key Words: The Bible, by Julian Charley

50
KEY WORDS
COMPARATIVE
RELIGION

by
ERIC J. SHARPE

JOHN KNOX PRESS
RICHMOND, VIRGINIA

INTERNATIONAL STANDARD BOOK NUMBER: 0–8042–3897–9
LIBRARY OF CONGRESS CATALOG CARD NUMBER: 70–161840

PRINTED IN GREAT BRITAIN

LIST OF WORDS

		Page
1.	Ancestor-worship	1
2.	Animism	2
3.	Astrology	4
4.	Birth and Death	5
5.	Community	7
6.	Comparative Method	8
7.	Creation	10
8.	Divination	11
9.	Dream	13
10.	Eschatology	15
11.	Evil	16
12.	Fate	18
13.	Fertility	19
14.	Festival	21
15.	God	22
16.	Heaven and Earth	24
17.	Hero	26
18.	Image	27
19.	Incarnation	29
20.	Initiation	31
21.	Judgement	32
22.	Life after Death	34
23.	Magic	35
24.	Mana	37
25.	Mission	38
26.	Mystery	40
27.	Mysticism	42

28.	Myth	43
29.	Phenomenology of Religion	45
30.	Prayer	47
31.	Priest	49
32.	Prophet	50
33.	Religion	52
34.	Revelation	54
35.	Ritual	55
36.	Sacred	57
37.	Sacrifice	59
38.	Salvation	60
39.	Sanctuary	62
40.	Scripture	64
41.	Shaman	65
42.	Sin	67
43.	Soul, Spirit	69
44.	Syncretism	70
45.	Tabu	72
46.	Theism (and derivatives)	73
47.	Time	75
48.	Totem	76
49.	Witchcraft	78
50.	Worship	80

INTRODUCTION

This book is intended to serve as a compact and elementary work of reference for those who are relative newcomers to the comparative study of religion. Like other fields of study, comparative religion already has an extensive technical vocabulary, and the student needs to know this vocabulary before he or she can proceed to the more advanced literature. In the pages which follow, the major technical terms are defined, together with a number of key concepts found, in one form or another, in the main Christian and non-Christian religious traditions. In such a wide field the choice of fifty key words must of necessity be somewhat arbitrary, but it is hoped that the words chosen will demonstrate a fair consistency of approach to the subject.

It should, however, be emphasized that this is not a dictionary of "world religions": terms such as "Christianity", "Hinduism", "Buddhism" and "Islam" have not been included, although a certain number of illustrative examples from world religions will be found. No attempt has been made to deal with any specific religious tradition as a whole. Other books and dictionaries on the market have been compiled with this particular end in view.

The term "comparative religion" is not without its difficulties, and more than one opinion is possible concerning its precise meaning. Here it is taken to mean the (as far as possible) objective study of religious beliefs and practices, ancient and modern, along historical and analytical lines. The precise methods by which this study may be undertaken vary greatly, but the following key words may perhaps serve to provide at least some rudimentary guidance in what has always been a necessary, and what is currently in process of becoming a highly popular, subject.

Numbers at the end of articles refer to other relevant articles.

Eric J. Sharpe

The University of Lancaster
England

1 **ANCESTOR-WORSHIP:** Among so-called "primitive" peoples the family unit is much stronger and more extensive than is usual in modern Western society. The unit comprises not only the living, but also, to some extent, the deceased members of the family. The practice of what is commonly called ancestor-worship is partly an expression of that solidarity, and partly linked with the idea that the soul of the ancestor, having been freed from the bonds of space and time, requires to be propitiated in order not to return and harm the living. These two motives of respect and fear are closely connected, and it is not possible to say which of them, if either, is the more original or the more important.

The earliest evidence of an apparent cult of dead ancestors comes from the Palaeolithic period; a number of cave and other burials have been found, some dating from the emergence of *homo sapiens*, in which it appears that the corpse has been interred in an occupied cave, equipped with a variety of grave goods, and protected (or restrained) in a variety of ways, for instance by the binding of the limbs. There in fact exists a practically unbroken custom among pre-literate peoples of equipping the dead with the necessities of life beyond the grave, of carrying out regular rituals at the grave-side or in the home in order to ensure the continued benevolence of his or her spirit, and at the same time of taking precautions to prevent the return of the ghost. The nineteenth-century writer Herbert Spencer put forward the theory that such practices as these were nothing less than the origin of all religion. Gods, he held, developed out of the ghosts of departed ancestors.

In many later cultures there is evidence of care and reverence for the spirits of the ancestors. Sometimes the motive of fear appears to predominate; often, however, fear gives way to genuine reverence. Even among pre-literate peoples, this may lead to unexpected sophistication, as in the beliefs of Australian Aborigines concerning the *Alcheringa*, or "dream-time", when

I

the first ancestors roamed and hallowed the earth. Where the ancestors are believed to be enjoying an ideal existence in a "heaven", elaborate rituals often exist for the maintaining of contact with them: the Vedic *shraddha* sacrifices, still offered by orthodox Hindus, are a case in point. Ancestor-worship was also of incalculable importance in Chinese religion, from whence it passed over to Japan, and to Shinto. As well as its established place in Japanese traditional religion, the ancestors are revered in some modern Japanese sects.

In the Judaeo-Christian tradition, ancestor-worship has had little place, apart from traces of an ancient cult of the dead in parts of the Old Testament. However, certain aspects of it have passed over into the popular cult of the saints in some branches of Christianity.

(2, 5, 17, 22, 43, 48)

2 **ANIMISM** is a word associated particularly with the name of the anthropologist E. B. Tylor; by it he meant "the belief in Spiritual Beings", and this he held to be both a "minimum definition of Religion" and the origin of all religion. The word was not, however, coined by Tylor, but by the German scientist G. E. Stahl in the early eighteenth century to describe the idea that every physical organism is permeated and controlled by an *animus*, or mind. Tylor took over Stahl's term to describe what he took to be the earliest and most primitive stage in the evolution of religion. The theory, as he sketched it out in his book *Primitive Culture* (1871), involved several different layers of belief: (*a*) belief in the existence of a non-material part of man (soul or spirit); (*b*) belief in the continued existence of the human soul, or souls, after death; (*c*) belief in the ability of the soul to leave the body, in states of dream or trance, for longer or shorter periods; (*d*) by

extension, the belief that animals, birds, plants and even "inanimate" objects also have souls; and (e) the belief in the existence of independent spirits, whether ghosts or not, having no connection with any person, creature or object. These beliefs Tylor regarded as having arisen as the result of a process of conscious reflection on the data of sense-experience.

Although the theory included genuine insights, it also had weaknesses. It assumed that primitive man was a thoroughgoing rationalist, and ignored the irrational elements in religion. It was also dependent on an *a priori* theory of religious evolution, in which it was axiomatic that lower forms always precede and develop into higher forms of religion. In this case it was assumed than animism developed, by a gradual process of personification, into polydaemonism and polytheism, which in its turn developed into monotheism. However, belief in spirits has (as far as our evidence goes) always been accompanied by belief in "high gods" – gods of the sky and atmosphere, owing nothing to the belief in souls or spirits for their genesis.

It is therefore necessary to reject the animistic theory as a hypothesis of the *origins* of religion, simply because it ignores too many of the available facts concerning the religion of pre-literate man. However, this is not to say that the term may not still serve a useful *descriptive* function with regard to the beliefs of pre-literate man concerning the soul. It is also common in some quarters to characterize the religious beliefs of pre-literate peoples as "animism" – a procedure which is perhaps permissible, provided that due account is taken of the limitations of the term, and provided that it is not supposed that it denotes a uniform system of beliefs and practices.

(1, 4, 9, 22, 41, 43)

3 ASTROLOGY, literally "the science of the stars", is bound up with the notion that the heavenly bodies exercise influence on the lives of human beings, either because they are themselves visible, though remote, deities, or by virtue of their own nature. The direct worship of sun, moon and stars is a well-attested phenomenon in many religions and in virtually all parts of the world. The observable regularity of their movements was believed to provide a key to the destiny of mankind, while the planets (wandering stars) exercised a peculiarly powerful influence, especially in conjunction with one another. On the one hand, therefore, the actual phenomena might be worshipped as divine; on the other, although worship was not excluded, an attempt might be made to study their motions and, on the hypothesis of the regularity of those motions, to predict the future.

Mesopotamia is traditionally regarded as the home of astrology, and there is little doubt that it spread from there in one direction into the Mediterranean world, and in the other into the Indian sub-continent. The Zodiac was known to the Mesopotamians from at least the eighth century B.C., and horoscopes were cast on the birth of children (the precise position of the planets at the moment of birth determining the fate of every person). In the Graeco-Roman world, the identification of the stars with traditional deities was taken over from Mesopotamia, the whole system being intimately connected with ideas concerning the nature of time, the nature of man, particularly his subjection to his fate, as written in the stars at the moment of his birth and the nature of deity. For instance, the stars and planets might be thought of as divine beings interposed between the Supreme Being and man; and man, if he was to ascend into the sphere of deity, had to pass through the spheres of the appropriate planets. Such schemes are common in Gnosticism and the mystery religions of the Hellenistic world. The New Testament, too, shows traces of this type of reasoning. The "principalities and powers" mentioned by Paul in e.g. 1 Cor. 6 and Gal. 4 were in all

4

likelihood astral forces, and from this source astralism and astrology passed into Western culture, where it survives, albeit in an attenuated form.

In India, astronomy/astrology (Sanskrit *jyotisa*) is one of the six *Vedangas*, or subsidiary sciences studied in traditional Hindu education. This was necessary partly in order to be able to fix days and hours for important sacrifices and festivals. Astrology is regarded as applied astronomy, i.e. a study of planetary movements which give good or bad results. The nine planets are significant objects of reverence in popular Hinduism. As in the Near East, it is believed that a careful study of the positions of the planets at the moment of birth can determine the whole course of a person's life; and in modern India and Ceylon, most marriages are arranged with reference to the compatibility of the two horoscopes concerned. It is also believed that there are auspicious and inauspicious times for all activities, such as setting out on journeys.

In view of the importance of astrology to the lives of many millions of people, and its close connection with concepts of deity, fate, and the nature of man, it has its given place within the comparative study of religion.

(4, 8, 12, 14, 15, 16, 26, 34, 47)

4 **BIRTH AND DEATH:** It has often been believed that the supernatural powers which control human destiny are especially active at certain critical points in man's life; among them, the most important are birth and death (others being initiation, marriage, etc.). The student of comparative religion will find many beliefs and many rituals (the so-called "rites of transition") connected with these critical points. The earliest of these may well date back to Palaeolithic times; among mankind's

earliest artifacts are crude figures of pregnant women, which may have been fertility charms, and which suggest that birth was a great mystery. The act of giving birth was hedged about with tabus, largely, it seems, because of the loss of blood which it involved. Both mother and infant were highly vulnerable at this time to the attentions of evil spirits, and rituals and charms were employed in order to ward off malevolent powers. Mother and child were ritually impure until such time as they had been received back into the community – the mother by a rite of purification, of which the Christian practice of "churching" is a relic, the child by naming, dedication, baptism or the like. Among primitive peoples and in folklore there are numerous other beliefs connected with childbirth – for instance the belief that the pains could be transferred to the husband (the phenomenon known as *couvade*, which can be explained in psychological terms). In societies where astrology is an active belief, great importance attaches to birth at an auspicious time, and an inauspicious birth might necessitate a symbolical "rebirth" – in India by passing the infant beneath the body of a cow.

On death, rituals were and are of several kinds, and the student can learn much from mortuary practices about essential religious beliefs. In religions of a fertility type, the body is usually buried (returned to the womb of mother earth); in religions where deities are mainly celestial, cremation is more common. In both cases, it has been usual to provide the dead man or woman with food, drink, weapons and servants for his or her continued life in the beyond. Such activities served a dual purpose: as acts of reverence, and as an insurance against the unwelcome attentions of a potentially malevolent ghost. In more highly developed religions, doctrines concerning the dead and the state of the dead may be added to or superimposed upon this more rudimentary stratum of belief. In primitive religion, death is never regarded as strictly "natural": it is always caused by malevolent powers, and involves final and irrevocable loss of soul. Consequently death may be personified, as a god, demon, angel or skeleton – or as "Father Time".

In religions growing out of, or influenced by, the Indian tradition, birth and death are recurrent on all levels of the phenomenal world. Nevertheless in popular belief, rituals guarding birth and death continue to be observed.

(22, 35, 43, 45)

5 **COMMUNITY:** Religion is seldom a purely individual concern. Usually it involves the individual in a distinctive relationship to a believing community. Originally the religious community was the family or clan or tribe, presided over by the paterfamilias or chief, who carried out priestly functions on behalf of the entire group. (It is not therefore necessary to follow Durkheim in regarding primitive religion simply as the apotheosis of the community.) The good of the individual was inextricably bound up with the good of the community, and beliefs and rituals were determined by and on behalf of the community, not by the individual in isolation. Similarly, in early urban settlements, the presence of the deity in his (or her) temple ensured the religious coherence of the community. This did not exclude individual devotion or piety, but it located it within a larger context.

In more recent times, although there have been strongly individualistic movements, and protests against various forms of religious collectivism, the community has been the chief means by which religious traditions have been maintained and transmitted. In India a *guru* (teacher) would gather a group of disciples, forming a small community, dedicated to the quest for reality. These developed in some cases into monastic institutions, adding a shared discipline and asceticism to the shared quest. The origins

7

of both Jainism and Buddhism are bound up with such ascetic communities. Similar movements are to be seen within Judaism, in which the Essenes and the early Christian Church represent extensions of this same principle of a teacher and his disciples. A similar pattern is observable in the case of Islam, which has always had the fundamental character of a community of obedience. In their later development, virtually all the great religions lay great stress on their communal character, though in many cases they tend in the course of time to develop into networks of interlocking communities, of which the Hindu caste system would be one good example. The larger community may remain something of an abstraction.

Commonly the emergence of one or another form of protest movement will involve the setting up of a "new community" with new ideals and new standards of belief and behaviour – often having the nature of *ecclesiola in ecclesia*, "a little church within the church". Monastic and semi-monastic communities (of either men or women) are found in Christianity, Hinduism and Buddhism.

For the student of comparative religion it is necessary constantly to weigh and evaluate the role of the individual believer against the community which supplies him with material for belief; neither can be fully understood without the other. The discipline of the sociology of religion, which concerns itself with the religious life and experience of man in community, has made great strides this century.

(1, 14, 35, 36, 50)

6 **COMPARATIVE METHOD:** The comparative method in historical studies came into prominence during the second half of the nineteenth century under the influence of evolutionary theory. In the study of religion, Friedrich Max Müller

8

stated the principle that, as in linguistic studies, "he who knows one, knows none", i.e. that the phenomena of religion could only be understood on a comparative basis, by the bringing together of material from diverse religious traditions. At first the main objects of comparative religion were twofold: (i) to elucidate the stages by which religion had evolved; (ii) to determine the nature of the genus, "religion", of which the separate religions are species. The first of these was greatly helped by data acquired from contemporary primitive peoples, understood through the theory of survivals as examples of earlier evolutionary stages. Notable names here were the anthropologists E. B. Tylor, A. Lang and J. G. Frazer in Britain, and Emile Durkheim and Lucien Lévy-Bruhl in France. This explicit reliance on comparative evolutionary method caused difficulties, however, and had the effect of alienating many theologians.

A further concern of comparative religion in its earliest phases was the problem of the origins of religion. But despite a plethora of theories, no satisfactory solution was reached.

Since the First World War, the evolutionary theory has been seriously called in question as an adequate presupposition for the study of religion. Most recent scholars have preferred to study separate religious traditions intensively, drawing comparisons only within areas in which historical dependence can be demonstrated. For that reason, the term "comparative religion" has often been expressly rejected, scholars preferring to speak of "the history of religions" or *Religionswissenschaft*. There are, however, signs that it may now be being accepted once more, partly due to the lack of any satisfactory alternative term.

All would agree that great care must be exercised when comparing religious phenomena, and that full account must be taken of all background factors – distinctive in every case. The comparison of religious systems or religions as a whole is seldom fruitful. A new discipline within comparative religion is known as the "phenomenology of religion" which seeks to understand by comparing "visible religion" (E. Lehmann), i.e. phenomena such as prayer, sacrifice, music and art.

In common parlance, "comparative religion" now denotes simply the comprehensive study of religions as phenomena in their own right, as far as possible without dogmatic presuppositions – though this ideal is not always realized.

(29, 33)

7 **CREATION:** Almost all major religions (the best-known exception being Buddhism) seek to account for the existence of the universe by means of doctrines of creation, usually cast in mythological form. Creation may be regarded as having taken place once for all, or as merely one in a number of creative acts, repeated in every cycle of the world's existence. Inevitably doctrines of creation are linked with doctrines and myths concerning the end of the world. The temporal process had a beginning; and it will have an end (or alternatively, many beginnings and ends).

The usual view is that before the cosmos was created, there existed some form of primal matter, but that this was unformed, in chaos; "the earth was without form, and void" (Gen. 1:2). This chaos may be hypostasized, as in the case of the Babylonian creation myth, as a dragon, or monster, Ti'amat. The myth then relates how the agent of creation (in the Old Testament, Yahweh, in the Babylonian account, Marduk) brought order out of chaos, either by an act of will or by a battle with the monster. Frequently in the ancient world the creation myth would serve a partly political purpose, in that it exalted the role of one god (usually the god of a city-state) over against other gods. The pattern, however, is constant: as a result of the work of some divine agent, the existing chaos is vanquished and order – the natural order – arises. Elsewhere creation myths may account for

10

the creation as the laying of an egg (Egypt), as the lifting up of a sunken world out of water (India), or as an act of self-propagation by a supreme deity (also India). Christian and Muslim theologians later interpreted this original material as implying creation *ex nihilo*, the only agent being the creative will of God (Allāh). In Buddhism and Jainism, which are in principle atheistic, there is no doctrine of creation, since the unending cycles of change which are assumed to underlie the natural order can be accounted for without recourse to a theory involving a creative Supreme Being.

It is now coming to be recognized that the function of some creation myths, as well as telling the story of creation, was to ensure the renewal of creation for a further cycle. They were thus repeated annually in the context of a ritual drama, as in ancient Mesopotamia and probably also elsewhere in the ancient Near East. It is in this context that Mircea Eliade has written of the myth of the "eternal return", i.e. a periodic return to the origins of the cosmos, as an escape from time and its uncertainties.

The creation myths of the ancient world are above all valuable sources for our understanding of the mind and world-view of ancient man. Their literal sense is less important than their overall conceptual framework, and it is in no case necessary to allegorize or spiritualize their contents as a condition of understanding.

(10, 14, 15, 28, 35, 47)

8 **DIVINATION** (from Latin *divinare*) means the attempt to discover, through non-human means, information about the course of future events. Such practices are extraordinarily widespread in the religious history of the world (a summary account covers fifty-five pages in Vol. 4 of the *Encyclopaedia of Religion and Ethics*), and, though commonly classified today as

superstition, have great tenacity. The underlying belief is that the course of human history is controlled by supernatural agencies only partly accessible to human influence. Where the controlling agency is a personal deity, then recourse may be had to prayer and sacrifice; but the frequency of divination increases in proportion as the supernatural powers become more remote. Where ultimate control is vested in an impersonal and immutable fate, man's only hope rests in being prepared for a pre-ordained course of events, which he cannot avoid, but may anticipate.

Also basic to the practice of divination is the belief that the supernaturals leave traces on the visible cosmos. Identity or correspondence between deities and the stars and planets gave rise to astrology. Information might also be derived from such sources as the flight of birds, the entrails (especially the liver) of a sacrificial animal, the cracks in a heated tortoise-shell, the appearance of the human body during sickness, and so on. Almost any observable phenomenon might become an omen. The patterns of thrown dice, bones, or sticks were taken to be a pattern of future events, when properly interpreted. The necessity for interpretation is similarly seen in the higher and more elaborate forms of divination, such as the oracles, of which the best known are those of ancient Greece – the Pythian oracle of Delphi and the oracle of Zeus at Dodona.

Any person or object which was "sacred" might mediate information concerning the future. Thus the practice of "incubation" – spending a night in a temple in order to receive a divine revelation – was resorted to in ancient Greece (compare Samuel's dream in 1 Sam. 3). Closely connected with this was the belief in the efficacy of dreams and trances as sources of contact with the supernatural. Holy scriptures have frequently been used for the same purpose; the practice of opening the Bible at random in order to discern the will of God has been known throughout the history of the Christian Church.

Since the dead have passed into the sphere of the sacred, a

12

further type of divination involves the conjuring up of the ghost of a powerful departed man or woman (necromancy). Book XI of Homer's *Odyssey* describes how Odysseus consults the soul of the dead Teiresias, and is informed of "the threads of destiny which the gods themselves have spun". In the Old Testament, Saul similarly learns of the future from the ghost of Samuel (1 Sam. 28).

A modified form of divination concerned the making of a choice between courses of action. The casting of lots and the tossing of a coin are forms of this practice. Many bishops were elected in the Middle Ages by such means.

Divination belongs, perhaps, to the periphery of religion, and has frequently been condemned by religious leaders. Nevertheless, it belongs formly within the area of belief in supernatural powers, and since it touches upon matters of intimate personal concern, it has proved difficult – if not impossible – to eradicate.

(3, 9, 12, 23, 34, 36, 47)

9 **DREAM:** In primitive belief, the experience of dreaming was one of a number of ways in which man was able to transcend the bounds of space and time. E. B. Tylor and others held that dream-experiences were one of the primary sources of religion, since these led man seriously to postulate the existence of a soul and hence of spirits. In fact many peoples can be shown to have a belief in more than one soul – the "free-soul" being that which wanders and holds converse with the spirits in the course of dreams. Such wanderings might on the one hand be restricted to the known world; but on the other, dreams might be a means of contact with the parallel world of the supernatural. The dead could reveal themselves in dreams; so, too, could the gods. Thus there was every reason to take seriously items of information communicated by these means.

13

Almost all ancient religions held dreams to be prophetic and revelatory. To the Greeks, dreams were sent directly from Zeus – at least to lords and kings: the dreams of other men had to be interpreted by specialists in the craft. In the literature of ancient Babylonia, Egypt and Israel there are frequent references to dreams as sources of divine revelation: some of the best known of these are in the Old Testament (Jacob's dream at Bethel, Gen. 28:10 ff., Joseph as a dreamer, Gen. 37:5 ff. and as an interpreter of dreams, Gen. 41:25 ff.), but in the Babylonian *Epic of Gilgamesh* the coming destruction of the world is revealed to Utnapishtim – the "Babylonian Noah" – in a dream, and the Babylonians in general laid great store by dreams and their interpretation. The Babylonian "Dream Books" ("If a date appears as a man's head, it means woe. If a fish appears on his head, that man will be strong," etc.) are the direct forerunners of such questionable literature today.

The likelihood of a revelatory dream increased if the place in which the individual slept were especially holy, i.e. the property of a specific deity. Thus to sleep in a temple or cult place was the likeliest way to experience a prophetic dream in answer to prayer. A "bad dream", wherever dreamed, would call for protective measures such as those specified, for ancient India, in parts of the *Atharva Veda*.

Broadly speaking, wherever belief in the objective reality of the supernatural world is still held, belief in the possibility of supernatural communication through the medium of dreams may follow. There is recent evidence on this point from, for example, the Christian Church in parts of Africa. Elsewhere the process of secularization tends to relegate the whole matter to the level of superstition, while the psychologist has replaced the priest as the only interpreter of dreams.

(2, 8, 12, 15, 34, 43)

10 ESCHATOLOGY, from the Greek word *eschatos*, "last", means "the teaching concerning the last things", or "the doctrine of the end". It may in some cases be taken, incorrectly, to refer to man's belief in a future life, heaven and hell (as in the *Concise Oxford English Dictionary*), but its correct meaning has to do with the end, not of the life of the individual, but of the existence of the world as we know it. Eschatology always presupposes a "protology", i.e. a doctrine of the beginning. Those religions which teach, or have taught, that the world will come to an end, also teach that the world has been created by divine action. The end of the present order is also the prelude to the creation of "new heavens and a new earth", i.e. to the re-establishment of the conditions which obtained when the world was first created.

It is often held that there is a profound difference in principle between "Eastern" and "Western" eschatologies. So, for example, the Judaeo-Christian view of a single act of creation leads inexorably to a single act of destruction and restoration, while in Indian thought, protology and eschatology have their place in an infinite series of such acts. This is, however, only partly true, since both conceive of eschatology as a beginning, as well as an end. Common to all eschatological myths is the belief that the process has happened before – by fire, flood, famine, earthquake or some other catastrophe – and that it is sure to happen again, perhaps soon (2 Pet. 3, cf. Gen. 6–8).

The end of the world in Indian thought is seen as the culmination of a mechanical process, following on a long decline in righteousness. It is proper here to speak of natural eschatology. Similar views are found in some Greek philosophies, such as those of Plato and the Stoics, and in certain primitive cultures. In Semitic (including Judaeo-Christian) thought, the end of the world comes about by the express will of the deity: the present order is brought to an end, the dead are raised and judged, evil is abolished and the new order inaugurated.

The source of virtually all eschatological ideas is probably to be seen in early cultic practices, and particularly in the various forms of annual festival, at which creation was symbolically dissolved into chaos and re-established for another year. Eschatology therefore need not be an expression of human pessimism, although it certainly reflects man's sense of dependence on powers beyond himself.

In modern religions, especially in the West, eschatology has tended to be emphasized somewhat less strongly, being replaced in many instances by optimistic doctrines of progress and evolution. However, it remains an important feature of many Christian and other sects. This all-pervasive element in ancient religions must however be interpreted on its own terms; previous failure to do so is a weakness which the comparative study of religion is only now beginning to overcome.

(7, 15, 21, 22, 28, 35, 47)

11 **EVIL** in the comparative study of religion is to be understood as all that makes man's tenure of the earth uncomfortable and insecure: notably suffering and death, though natural catastrophes may also be included. Man's attempts to come to terms with, and to explain, the problem of evil constitute a central part of his religious and moral consciousness.

The most widespread explanation of evil in the ancient religions ascribes it either to the unfathomable will of God or the gods, or to a rigid law of cause and effect in which all evil is caused by human sins and failings, sometimes known, sometimes not. Thus in ancient Mesopotamia, where man was believed to be virtually the slave of the gods, suffering and death had been brought about because the gods willed it, and man's quest for immortality was doomed to failure, again because of the express will of the gods. In primitive societies generally, however, disease and death were held to be caused by the action of evil spirits; any breach of tabu and any failure to maintain good relations with the spirit-world might lead to dire consequences for the individual. The problem in such cases was not to account for evil, but to discover, and if possible to neutralize, its precise cause by magical means.

The relationship between concepts of deity and the problem of evil may be expressed in one of two main ways: either by means of an ambivalent conception of deity, in which opposites and contradictions are subsumed (a typical example of this would be seen in the Hindu god Shiva), or by postulating a dualistic scheme, in which good and evil are both personified as independent and antagonistic powers (the best example being the dualism of Ahura Mazda and Angra Mainyu in ancient Iranian religion). A similar dualism is seen in Christianity, in which Satan has in the past been seen as an independent agent, tolerated by God for the limited period of this present world, but doomed to final destruction.

The Indian religious tradition explains the problem of evil on strictly logical lines, claiming that all suffering is deserved, and must bring its own retribution in a future life (the doctrine of *karma*). But since all existence implies suffering – the Buddhist position *par excellence* – man's proper quest is to attempt to escape altogether from the phenomenal order, and hence from evil.

Common to many traditions is the belief that man is able to choose between good and evil, and that suffering is thus a consequence of human free will. Salvation is therefore, among other things, liberation from suffering by means of obedience to the will of a God who is utterly opposed to evil. The problem of the existence of evil remains, however, giving rise to the further problem of theodicy – the accounting for the motives of an all-loving and all-powerful God who nevertheless "allows" evil.

(12, 15, 19, 21, 37, 38, 42)

12 FATE (Destiny): The belief in fate – an inscrutable power directing the affairs of man in the world – is found to a varying degree in most human cultures. If we take "destiny" to mean broadly that which happens to men individually or collectively, these events may take place as a result of the will of God or the gods, as a result of the working of impersonal forces ("fate" proper), or by random chance. Where deity is involved, there is some possibility of altering one's destiny, by prayer, sacrifice, etc., but where fate is genuinely an impersonal power, then no measures can be taken to avert its outworkings, except perhaps to make use of methods of divination in order to prepare oneself. But as Ringgren has pointed out (*Fatalistic Beliefs*, 1967, p. 8) these two attitudes may occur in one and the same religion, and even in one and the same person.

The problem for the student of comparative religion is to determine to what extent fate is a power exercised by specific gods, and to what extent it operates independently of the gods, even over the gods. Some scholars (e.g. Widengren, Pettazzoni) hold that the idea of an independent, impersonal fate is a later development, fate being originally a function of a deity. Very often the development of language and popular usage has led to this view, particularly when the high god as Determiner of Destiny (Pratt's term) has become somewhat remote. A similar shift in meaning may have taken place in respect of such terms as "fortune", which in some cultures can be shown to have originally denoted a personal guardian spirit, but which comes to mean an abstract quality of well-being and luck.

In any given religious tradition, it is likely that the gods as arbiters of destiny will share the field with more or less abstract conceptions of impersonal fate, according to the presuppositions of individuals. Sometimes the one is stronger, sometimes the other. Christianity, for instance, denies strongly that there can be an impersonal fate independent of God; in Islam, Allāh is the only arbiter of destiny. In old Scandinavian religion, fate may be

18

regarded as completely impersonal, ultimately controlling even the gods, but it may also be personified or regarded as being spun by the Norns. A curiously ambivalent attitude is found in Hinduism, where on the one hand the destiny of man is held to be controlled almost entirely by the influence of the stars – a further dimension of the concept of fate in other areas also – but where on the other hand man's present status is due to the influence of the good and bad *karma* which he has accumulated in previous existences.

It appears that there is a primary conflict here (and elsewhere) between official religious doctrine and the fundamental human instincts, the former insisting on some form of moral causation of that which man experiences, the latter feeling that the nature of ultimate control is inexplicable. The relationship between these two attitudes would provide a very fruitful field for further research.

(3, 8, 15, 47)

13 **FERTILITY** refers in comparative religion, first to the principle of reproduction and growth in man, animals and plants, and secondly to the belief that reproduction and growth can be controlled and furthered by magical or religious means. The religions of the past contain many fertility rituals, some of which have survived to our day, though in an attenuated form.

In the past, it was believed that fertility was entirely controlled by the inhabitants of the spirit-world, who were able to give and withhold life. In this area of human experience, there was no effect without its spiritual cause. The world was governed by laws – not scientific, but no less rigid for that – and it was up to man to adjust himself to those laws.

The pattern of fertility was first of all cyclical: in it, growth followed birth, maturity followed growth, and death followed maturity. But these cycles were controlled by spirits and gods, any one of which could be dangerous if slighted. Thus primitive and archaic religion was very largely concerned with man's attempts to control the power wielded by the supernaturals. In agricultural communities, special rituals were concerned with the sowing of seed and with the harvest, while lesser festivals took place at midsummer and midwinter. In all cases the objective was to ensure a good and fertile year.

The ancient religions also believed in a close and elaborate correspondence between man and the cosmos. It was therefore appropriate for the king and the priestess to further the fertility of the fields by an act of intercourse (Babylonia) – a pale shadow of the "sacred marriage" surviving in the West in some Maytime rituals.

Fertility was ultimately controlled by the high god of the sky, e.g. the Greek Zeus, the Roman Jupiter, the Scandinavian Thor. In the Old Testament we find: "The eyes of all look to thee, and thou givest them their food in due season . . ." (Ps. 145:15, cf. 147:8) But the lesser gods and spirits also had their proper areas of influence, while in some parts of the world the fertility of man is thought to be controlled by the influence of ghosts, or by spirits dwelling in the dampest part of the forest (the link between water and fertility is obvious). Mythology and folklore from many parts of the world show that the supernaturals were responsible for providing water for man, beast and field. In Derbyshire (England) the custom of "well-dressing" is still practised – evidently a survival of belief in supernatural guardians of the wells, who had to be honoured lest he (or she) should cause the well to run dry.

The mythology of fertility may make use of a variety of forms of expression: sky-father and earth-mother, husband and wife, bull and cow, mother and child. These symbols have undergone many modifications in the course of the centuries, but are still in many cases recognizable. In some instances, a fertility cult may

20

develop into a cult of salvation, and acquire a still more complex mythology (e.g. the Greek Eleusinian Mysteries); in such cases, the figure of a mother-goddess who is at the same time a goddess of the dead is usually prominent.

(14, 16, 22, 26, 35, 38, 47)

14 FESTIVAL: By "festival" is understood here the periodical dramatic representation in solemn forms of an episode or episodes from sacred history or mythology, with a view to the perpetuation of their effectiveness for another longer or shorter period of time.

Of religion in its social aspect we may say "in the beginning was the drama". Religion was originally not so much thought out or prayed out as acted out, and in archaic religions there is a close link between magic, myth and ritual. Concerning the earliest forms of this link we can only speculate, but by the time of the first civilizations (*a*) the well-being, order and balance of society was believed to rest in the hands of the gods, (*b*) seasonal rituals (festivals) were carried out in order to retain the favour of the gods and to renew the cosmic order, (*c*) the myths of the gods provided a "libretto" for the festivals and (*d*) the dramatic action of the festival involved a hierarchy of participants, with the king at their head. The greatest of these festivals took place at the New Year, where the great creation myths were often recited.

In time the bond between myth and ritual was relaxed, and numbers of lesser festivals developed, though always with some mythological content, and always with reference to a natural cycle – seasonal, solar, lunar, annual. The purpose of religious festivals is to re-enact (subsequently to call to mind) episodes in sacred history, to do honour to a sacred person (god, goddess, king, saint, martyr) and ultimately to maintain the sacred rhythm.

21

However, it is possible for the outward forms of a festival to survive when its original purpose has fallen into obscurity.

The major festivals thus centred on a cultic drama bound up
with the great natural rhythms of birth, growth, life and death,
the conflict between light and darkness, and the need to secure the
benevolence of the supernatural powers ultimately responsible
for the maintenance of this order. The drama was clearly connected with the status of man in the world, and, in those areas in
which religion gradually became more and more anthropocen-
tric, festivals changed in quality. The drama of the changing seasons gave place to the drama of man's salvation – though often
with a remnant of seasonal observance. The Christian Easter is a
spring festival, just as Christmas preserves a great deal of the pre-
Christian midwinter festival of the sun. Christian saints took over
the attributes, and festivals, of pre-Christian minor deities.
The seasonal nature of the festival calendar is as apparent in
classical Christianity as it is in classical Hinduism, and for substantially the same reasons.

In the history of religion, the intensive observance of festivals is
part of the agricultural way of life, and the growth on the personal
level of intellectualization and on the social level of urbanization
can be shown to have modified this dramatic concern. Intellectual
religion, of whatever type, is timeless in the sense of being un-
concerned with cycles of time, and ethical principles take the
place of a sense of dependence upon supernatural powers.

(7, 13, 26, 31, 35, 37, 47, 50)

15 **GOD** (Deity): It is a truism to say that the question of belief in
God or the gods is determinative for most historical religions.
Comparative religion is not, however, concerned to decide
which god, if any, is the true God, or to dismiss all belief in deity

22

as an illusion (though both approaches have been known under the guise of comparative religion). As a descriptive and analytical science, comparative religion is concerned to observe and analyse the full range of man's beliefs concerning the unseen and supernatural world, suspending judgement as to the adequacy or otherwise of those beliefs.

The past hundred years or so have seen many attempts to trace the origins of belief in God. Until fairly recently the commonest approach was to trace out an evolutionary pattern in religion, beginning with belief in impersonal powers (animatism) or spirits (animism), and continuing through polydaemonism, polytheism and henotheism to ethical monotheism. An opposite theory, favoured by some theologians, saw the lower forms of belief in God as degeneration from a primeval monotheism. Another important theory, put forward by Rudolf Otto, suggested that an irrational sense of "the numinous" (Lat. *numen*, deity) was the earliest form of religion.

It is now known that many materially "primitive" peoples have held a belief in an ethical creator-god, usually identified with, or living in, the sky (a so-called "high god"), and some scholars have now begun to suggest that the belief in high gods (German *Hochgottglaube*) was the earliest unitary form of religious belief. On this view, polytheism resulted from the personification of various attributes of the high god, monotheism as we know it developing out of polytheism. This is, however, pure speculation, and the historical evidence is that man seems always to have believed in a graded hierarchy of supernatural beings, from the high gods of the sky and atmosphere down to the ghosts and demons infesting the earth.

In religious belief, lines of demarcation have been drawn at various points across this hierarchy: above the line, gods and goddesses; below it, ghosts and demons, to be treated with care, but not worshipped. And even rigidly monotheistic religions (such as Islam) do not altogether deny the existence of the lower orders, though the modern tendency is to discount them as products of popular superstition. At the other extreme, apparently atheistic philosophies, such as Samkhya and Buddhism, do not deny the existence of supernatural beings as such: the gods exist, but are bound by the same rigid laws as men. What is denied in each case is the existence of a Supreme Being outside the judicial system of *karma*.

Within most great religions the main theological points at issue are whether God is to be regarded as personal or impersonal, whether he is exclusively male, and whether he is transcendent (beyond the world) or immanent (within the world). Also of central importance is the way in which God has communicated with man – i.e. the doctrine of revelation. In some religions, especially Christianity and Hinduism, the question of incarnation is also central. But the student will find that almost every question of religious belief and practice goes back ultimately to the nature of belief in God, and cannot be fully understood apart from the doctrine of God or the gods.

(*passim*)

16 **HEAVEN AND EARTH:** In archaic religions, life is very often seen as being influenced by pairs of opposites, and as subject to the tension and interaction between them. The polarity of light and darkness, night and day, summer and winter, life and death represented the principle of conflict; the complementarity of man and woman, male and female the principle of interaction. Man's life, according to primitive cosmologies, was lived between heaven and earth – both highly concrete entities, and both divine. Thus it may be that mankind's first deities were personifications of the sky and the earth, the primeval pair of the sky-father and the earth-mother, out of whose fruitful union were

born the living creatures. It is pointless to argue primacy for either partner; quite apart from the lack of evidence neither could be complete without the other. Nor can very much be deduced from the variety of names given to heaven and earth in ancient mythologies, least of all concerning the diffusion of the idea: in ancient religions, the world over, the primeval pair are simply there.

The personification of the sky as a deity (or the idea of a deity living in the sky) is known in comparative religion as a "high god". Such gods have been worshipped from time immemorial as guardians of the cosmic order, as creators, as arbiters of destiny and as givers of fertility (senders of rain). Hunting and nomadic peoples generally appear to have worshipped deities connected with the sky and with other atmospheric phenomena – wind, storm, thunder, lightning, etc. The earth could equally well be worshipped under a divine aspect as mother, as the one from whose body living creatures are born and nourished. The earth is the divine body, fertilized by the rain as the divine seed – a macrocosmic parallel to human intercourse. Peoples whose livelihood has depended entirely on the earth have often tended to honour the earth-mother rather than the sky-father.

These two types of religion, celestial and chthonic (earth-centred), have other characteristics. In the former, for instance, the dead may be thought of as living with the gods in a celestial paradise, and cremation may be more common; in the latter, the dead dwell underground, and the bodies of the dead are buried.

It should be emphasized, however, that the two types are seldom or never found in absolute isolation. In historical religions the polarity of heaven and earth is filled in with a multitude of intermediate beings, gods and spirits of the air and atmosphere, local gods and goddesses, functional deities, and the spirits of the dead. Cosmology becomes steadily more complex, with a corresponding complexity in notions of deity. Nevertheless, there are modern religions in which the primary polarity is still very much in evidence. Hindu gods and goddesses often have celestial and chthonic characteristics respectively, while the reflection of the human microcosm is seen in the words of the Hindu marriage ritual, where the bridegroom says to the bride, "I am heaven, you are the earth."

(4, 7, 10, 13, 21, 22, 28)

17 HERO: The word "hero" is derived from the Greek *hērōs*, used in some contexts to denote an intermediate stage between a god and a man. Elsewhere it refers to the great men of the past: the Age of Heroes was Hesiod's fourth age of man. Although today the word is used vaguely to mean anyone admired for his unusual attainments, in comparative religion it retains something of these two original senses.

There is ample evidence in the history of religion that great figures in the history of a particular tribe or people have after their deaths been accorded divine or semi-divine honours. Often there is little to distinguish in principle hero-worship from ancestor-worship; but where the individual in question has been responsible for some important cultural advance or discovery, the degree of reference increases in proportion. Examples of the worship of "culture-heroes" are found from all parts of the ancient world. Although hero-worship was centred on the tomb of the departed, the culture-hero's cult was not so limited. An interesting type of culture-hero is found in the mythology of some North American Indian tribes, who revere a mischievous, paradoxical demiurge, who may have theriomorphic characteristics, or may be more human. He taught men much mischief, but also taught them the use of fire, flint and tobacco. He is often called "the Trickster", and similar combinations of qualities are found in deities from other parts of the world, e.g. in the Scandinavian figure of Loki.

It has sometimes been held, mistakenly, that the worship of departed heroes was the earliest form of religion. This theory was first put forward in the third century B.C. by Euhemeros, in his novel *The Sacred Inscription* (whence the name "Euhemerism"), and it is found in Cicero, the Church Fathers, Snorri Sturluson, David Hume and Herbert Spencer.

The greatest difficulty which the student finds in this area is that of distinguishing between "gods", heroes and other spirits as the recipients of divine honours. Often there is little to distinguish heroes from gods, or from saints. Sometimes there seems no historical basis for hero-cults (the Trickster being a case in point); on other occasions the historical basis is clear, as in some of the epic heroes of the Indo-European peoples. Always there are deep layers of mythological interpretation between the "original" figure (always supposing there to have been one) and the figure of popular reverence.

So while on the one hand we must accept the tendency for myth to gather round a subject of popular admiration, on the other we have to recall the hierarchical structure of the supernatural world in the mind of archaic man. The hero had his place in this scheme, but it was a place far inferior to that of the high god, and the powers at his disposal were far less. For this reason, hero-*worship* might often be a misnomer, since reverence scarcely amounted to worship in the fullest sense.

(1, 19, 34, 50)

18 **IMAGE:** Man's desire to represent deities in visible and tangible form, by sculpture, painting or drawing, can be traced back to Palaeolithic times. From the very first, images (or icons, from Greek *eikōn*; the word "idol" is pejorative) have been more than mere representations, and have been believed to contain

within themselves, by derivation, supernatural power. The image was thus a sacred object – not so much by virtue of its form as from the act of consecration which "breathed life" into it. As such it served a variety of purposes.

In temples, worship centres on a cult-image, which may be realistic or entirely symbolical. This image is given the honours which the worshipper feels are due to the deity. It is treated as a living and breathing being (often on the analogy of a king), which is awakened, washed, fed, holds audience and finally retires each day. To the ordinary worshipper it *is* the deity, though it may be argued that it is really the form in which the deity has chosen to reveal himself in that place. At certain seasons the image is taken out of the temple and carried around the particular territory belonging to the deity.

Smaller images may be carried or worn by devotees. Again, these possess power. Some represent the deity, others the deity's particular symbol (Shiva's *lingam*, Thor's hammer, the Christian cross). As well as images of deity, images and symbols of saints may be worn or carried in the same way.

Although image-worship and veneration has been, and still is, widespread (most ancient religions, Hinduism, Buddhism, Catholic and Orthodox Christianity), many religions either condemn the making of images of deity, or contain within themselves anti-iconic groups (Judaism, Islam, Protestant Christianity). This may be a matter of reaction against what is held to be worship directed to the wrong object, or a conviction that since no image can possibly correspond to the divine reality, no image should be made. Against this view it is argued, for example by Hindus (there are anti-iconic groups in Hinduism) that the image serves to concentrate the mind on a deity admittedly infinitely greater than the image.

The making of images today is taken to be the application of plastic symbolism to the concept of deity. Popular belief, it is argued, looks upon the image in magical or semi-magical

28

categories, but on the level of symbolism, to reject the use of images is merely to opt for alternative forms of symbolism, usually verbal. This is, however, to presuppose a shift of emphasis in religious belief and practice, from the application of supernatural power to the intellectual appreciation of symbols. Throughout the greater part of the religious history of mankind the image has served, not only as a symbol (in the modern sense of that word) but as a focus of sacredness and a repository of the very power wielded by the god represented. In this sense the instinct of popular belief may be closer to the age-old motive for making images than is the intellectual attitude of modern man.

(23, 35, 39, 48, 50)

19 **INCARNATION:** Incarnation, literally "the taking of bodily form", may apply to the form or forms taken by any soul or spirit, but in comparative religion is generally taken to mean the assumption of human or animal form by a deity. It is necessary to distinguish incarnation from spirit-possession, in which the body is believed to be temporarily invaded and controlled by an otherwise independent spirit. At times, however, it may be difficult to distinguish the one belief from the other, or to decide at what point possession becomes incarnation. In Christian theology, for instance, the belief that the body of Jesus was temporarily possessed by the Spirit of God (from baptism to crucifixion) is officially classed as a heresy.

In many ancient mythologies, stories were told of the way in which specific deities had revealed themselves in human or animal form in order to attain particular human ends. The commonest of these was the desire for intercourse with humans. Here incarnation was merely a device for explaining the source of divine qualities in some individuals or families. Zeus in particular had many human offspring in this way. To speak of a king as "son of god" often implied belief in divine parentage.

The two religions in which the belief in incarnation has been most highly developed are Hinduism and Christianity. There are, however, important differences between the two, although both presuppose the decline of moral values and the restoration of a divine order – a notable development over the archaic mythologies. In Hindu thought, the belief in incarnations (Sanskrit, *avatars*) is seen in its typical form in Vaishnavism. Vishnu as Supreme Being takes a variety of forms in order to deliver the world from catastrophe. In the cyclical view of time which dominates Indian thought, every successive age (*yuga*) has its own incarnation, among them Rama, Krishna and the Buddha – with one incarnation still to come. A similar view is found in Mahāyāna Buddhism.

The Christian doctrine of incarnation, which developed out of Jewish Messianic speculation, differs from the Indian view in that the incarnation of God in Jesus Christ has taken place one and for all time, an act of re-creation corresponding to the original act of creation. It presupposes a linear, rather than a cyclical view of time, and the incarnation inaugurates a totally new age in human history, rather than being an *ad hoc* solution to a temporary problem. An attempt at combining the two views is found in some Gnostic sects, in which Abraham, Isaac, Jacob and Christ are all regarded as periodic incarnations, not of God, but of Adam.

Incarnation as a problem within the study of religion assumes a prior doctrine of God, and a particular view of the temporal process. It is also central to doctrines of salvation and of the nature and destiny of man. Of the great religions, only Judaism and Islam deny the occurrence of direct incarnations of God, though some Shi'a Muslims hold the *imāms* to have been "points of divine manifestation".

(1, 17, 28, 38, 47)

20 INITIATION denotes the ritual by which a person is received into full membership of any community or society. Rites of initiation are the most clearly defined of the so-called "rites of transition" (*rites de passage*) which mark the passage of the individual from one form or stage of life to another; others include rites in connection with birth, marriage and death. There are few societies or fellowships which do not make use of some form of initiation ceremony. The religious significance of some of these is questionable, but among pre-literate peoples and in explicitly religious societies, initiation implies an altered relationship to God or the gods, frequently expressed in elaborate symbolism.

The usual time for initiation among primitive peoples is at puberty, when the young man or woman ceases to be a child and becomes a full adult member of the tribe. Circumcision and sub-incision may take place, and various tests may also be imposed, particularly upon young men as demonstrations of manhood. In some primitive societies (e.g. among some North American Indians), the youth had in some way to enter into a relationship with a personal guardian spirit. The young person would also be taught the religious lore of the tribe (often hidden from women, children and strangers), and might be given a new name. Taken as a whole, the ritual would often symbolize death and rebirth.

This same understanding of initiation as rebirth is found in the great religions. The three highest classes of Hindu society (Brahman, Kshatriya, Vaishya) are known as "twice-born" for this very reason. In Christianity, too, baptism is interpreted as a resurrection to new life (e.g. Rom. 6:4). This same motif is found in the Hellenistic mystery religions, and in Gnosticism. The giving of a new name – often indicating the deity to which the individual now belongs – is part of the symbolism of new birth. This applies at whatever stage of life the initiation takes place. Christian initiation may take place within a few days of birth, and "Christening" of course involves the giving of a name; but when initiation occurs later in life – as for instance on conversion from another religion – a new Christian name may also be given. Otherwise, Christian initiation rites are usually now divided into two parts: (*a*) baptism and naming, followed at puberty by (*b*) confirmation or its equivalent.

To pass through an initiation ritual involves teaching, an act of purification, and a deliberate renunciation of the past ("the world, the flesh and the devil"), together with the taking of vows for the future. Thereupon the individual is free to take a full part in the cultic life of the group; he or she has been accepted by the society and its deity or deities. Further *rites de passage* may follow, in which the relationship with deity is intensified. Ordination and the entry into the religious life of a monk or a nun are examples of such higher initiations, in which substantially the above elements are present.

(4, 5, 26, 31, 36, 41)

21 **JUDGEMENT** (of the Dead): That the souls of the dead are judged after death is a belief found in some, but by no means all, religions. Where such a belief is found, it implies an assessment by a deity of the quality of the individual's life on earth, and an allotment of rewards and punishments accordingly.

Although in the beliefs of some pre-literate peoples the dead followed a road of some difficulty on the way to blessedness, the trials to be overcome were of a practical, rather than a moral, nature (e.g. the crossing of water, the choosing of alternative paths). As a rule, the state of the dead in the religions of pre-literate peoples is morally undifferentiated. This was also the case in the religions of the ancient Near East and Greece, where there was no belief in judgement.

The outstanding exception, and the earliest example of a belief in post-mortem judgement, is found in the religion of ancient Egypt (c. 2400 B.C.), in which the individual soul is morally assessed in the presence of the god Osiris. The heart of the deceased was weighed, and judgement was meted out on the basis of his ritual, ethical and legal merit. The Egyptian material is unique in the ancient world, and typifies one major form of belief in judgement – that in which the soul of the deceased is judged more or less immediately after death.

The second major form is connected closely with eschatological myths of the end of the world, and sees judgement as taking place collectively at the end of this present world order. The ultimate source of this view may have been Iran; it first appears in Judaism in the *Book of Daniel*; and it is found in developed form in both Christianity and Islam. In this view the end of the world is accompanied by a general resurrection of the dead, and their final separation into the just and the unjust (sheep and goats). Although the theme of the Last Judgement has been a powerful one in Christian history (particularly in the Middle Ages), in the popular mind it has often been replaced by belief in immediate judgement, on the Egyptian pattern. A further link with Egypt is provided by the medieval concept of the weighing of the soul, the scales being held by the archangel Michael.

In the Indian religious tradition, there is no belief in judgement after death. There is, however, belief in moral retribution. The law of *karma* by which the status of the individual is determined by his good and evil deeds in a previous incarnation, functions as a precise judicial system without a judge.

The nature of the rewards and punishments meted out to the soul has given rise in the popular imagination to elaborate myths of heavens, hells and purgatories. Heavens and hells are also found in the Indian tradition, though in this case only as temporary dwellings before the soul is reincarnated.

(4, 10, 22, 28, 43, 47)

22 LIFE AFTER DEATH: The belief that life continues in some form after the death of the body is found at the dawn of human history, and continues through all ages and all cultures. It has been one of the most important functions of religion to attempt to systematize this belief and to provide it with a mythological framework.

Palaeolithic man anticipated this future existence by placing food, ornaments and weapons in the grave. However, in the absence of other indications we do not know exactly how life after death was visualized, except that it was evidently a continuation of normal human life. The same applies broadly to neolithic cultures and to later pre-literate cultures. Among modern pre-literate peoples, beliefs in life after death are closely bound up with conceptions of the soul: neither is very consistent or very logical. So while on the one hand the soul might be thought to hover in the vicinity of the grave as a potentially dangerous ghost, on the other hand it might be on the way to some form of heaven, and might even be being reborn in a child.

Continued existence in or near the grave was expanded by the ancient Semitic peoples into a belief in a dusty, dismal existence, in which there was equality of misfortune, but neither deity nor joy. In Hebrew this is called *Sheol*; in Greece, where a similar belief obtained, *Hades*. An alternative and much more optimistic belief located the realm of the dead in the immediate presence of God or the gods, at least for the fortunate dead who could have the correct rituals performed, or who belonged to a favoured class. The celestial paradise of ancient Egypt, the Greek Elysian Fields, and the Norse Valhalla were all for the *élite* – kings, priests, warriors and the like. In time a certain democratization took place, particularly in the Hellenistic world. The so-called mystery religions offered blessedness in the hereafter to all initiates.

Common to all these views was the belief that only the soul lived on; the body perished. In India, belief in the immortality of the soul was always prominent, though in this case linked with belief in rebirth – not, however, a characteristic of early Vedic religion. The Judaeo-Christian tradition rejected the doctrine of the immortality of the soul, and held instead the idea of the resurrection of the entire human personality, body and soul, on the last day. In Christianity, in common with Zoroastrianism and Islam, the fullest form of life after death is restricted to those accepted by God. The remainder are condemned either to punishment or to annihilation.

Religious belief in life after death has in recent years been characterized as little more than pious wishful thinking, a form of compensation for the inequalities and injustices of life. However, such criticism takes little account of the actual circumstances of life after death in religious belief – often unpleasant and hopeless, or open to only a tiny *élite* among men. Although the mythological details of life after death clearly reflect local preoccupations, the belief as such is a valid protest against what must otherwise remain a terrible mystery.

(4, 10, 21, 43, 47)

23 **MAGIC** may be defined as the attempt on the part of an individual or group to influence a given course of events through the control or manipulation of supernatural forces. It differs from religion in that religion seeks to enter into a relationship with deity as the ultimate source of these same forces. The difference between religion and magic may therefore be little more than an attitude of mind: the boundary between the two may in specific instances be very indistinct, and one and the same action may be interpreted as both "religious" and "magical".

J. G. Frazer attempted, in *The Golden Bough*, to derive religion from magic, claiming that an age of magic preceded an age of religion in human history. This claim is without foundation. The evidence suggests rather that religion is apt to degenerate into magic than that magic is capable of developing into religion. Religious symbols – verbal, textual, iconic – are often used without reference to deity in a way which can only be described as magical.

Of more value is Frazer's distinction between two main types of magic, sympathetic magic and contagious magic. Sympathetic magic depends on the belief in the power of imitation to produce that which is imitated. Thus for a hunting tribe to arrange an imitation hunt, in which a certain animal is symbolically killed, is designed to ensure success when the hunt actually takes place. To pierce a wax doll with a pin produces pain in the person the doll represents. Contagious magic depends on the belief that an object which has once been in contact with a person can continue to affect that person in some way. Locks of hair, clothes, nail clippings and other possessions may serve in this way, while the knowledge of a person's name gives power over its bearer. However, it should be stressed that this distinction is not drawn by the magician, but by the analytical scholar.

A simpler distinction is between black and white magic. Black magic is designed to harm, white magic to help. Characteristic of black magic in some cultures is its use of religious symbols in the opposite sense from that which is proper and normal, e.g. in the so-called Black Mass.

A certain degree of confusion always attends the discussion of magic, even in the context of comparative religion. This is partly due to the extraordinary vagueness of the term in common parlance, partly to some of the factors already mentioned. However, if it can be accepted that magic is always an attempt on man's part to *control* supernatural power without relying on the mediation of a personal supernatural agency, then it may perhaps be separated in principle from religion. The real complications arise when it is observed, for instance, that certain ritual actions are believed to work *ex opere operato*, and that what is ostensibly a religious act, since gods are called upon, in reality is believed to work more or less automatically. In such cases the student ought seriously to question whether the accepted distinction between magical and religious action does not confuse the issue further, and whether the term "magic" ought not to be used very sparingly indeed.

(2, 8, 11, 35, 36, 41, 43, 49)

24 **MANA** is a word of Melanesian origin, meaning "supernatural power". It was introduced as a technical term into comparative religion by the anthropologist R. R. Marett, in connection with his theory of pre-animism or animatism. Marett's contention was that behind and prior to the "belief in spiritual beings" (animism) which Tylor had claimed to be the origin of religion, there was an ill-defined religious sense or instinct, made up of fear, wonder and admiration in face of what early man considered to be the supernatural. This he believed to be essentially an impersonal power, capable of manifesting itself in any unusual person or object, and to describe it he borrowed the term *mana*. *Mana* therefore was taken by Marett (and following him, by many other scholars) to mean an impersonal and uncanny power capable of being sensed, feared and reverenced by archaic man. As a theory of the origin of religion, this is usually called "animatism".

Marett's main informant concerning *mana* was R. H. Codrington, who had certainly claimed that it was an impersonal power. However, he had also pointed out that it was "always connected with some person who directs it; all spirits have it, ghosts generally, some men". To take a modern analogy, *mana* is neither more nor less impersonal than "genius", which may be (verbally) an abstract quality, but which cannot in practice even be envisaged apart from a person. *Mana*, in short, is now recognized to be a quality of the supernatural or sacred, and entirely dependent on the belief in the existence of the spiritual beings it was meant, in Marett's theory, to supersede. *Mana* was never worshipped: only persons and objects having affinity with the supernatural, and therefore possessing the quality of *mana*. Codrington had written: "All success and all advantage proceed from the favourable exercise of this *mana*; whatever evil happens has been caused by the direction of this power to harmful ends, whether by spirits, or ghosts, or men. In no case, however, does this power operate, except under the direction and control of a person – a living man, a ghost, or a spirit."

Marett's *mana*-hypothesis of the origin of religion is therefore mistaken, and the word itself should – like other "power-words" derived from other primitive cultural areas – only be used within the context of the area to which it properly applies, i.e. the area of Melanesian religious belief and practice. Its widespread use in comparative religion during the earlier part of this century has been an unfortunate example of the uncritical acceptance of the evolutionary hypothesis as applied to religious origins, and particularly of the possibility of discovering the origins of religion in the workings of the human mind.

(2, 36, 45)

25 **MISSION:** It is usual in the study of religion to distinguish between missionary (Latin *missio*, "sending") and non-missionary religions. Missionary religions consider that their basic tenets are of universal significance, and take steps to propagate those tenets outside the original company of believers; non-missionary religions lack this universal perspective. When a

religion is closely identified with the way of life of a specific ethnic group, and the concept of deity is of relevance only within that group, mission is neither desirable nor necessary, although culture-contacts (and particularly processes of conquest) may have the effect of mission. Missionary religions are usually held to have been those whose teachings have been promulgated by a founder or a prophet in such a way as to be potentially independent of the original situation in which proclamation took place. In the history of religion, however, such a sharp distinction cannot always be maintained. Beliefs and practices have been propagated in various ways, not all of them either conscious or deliberate. Wherever believers have come into contact with one another, discussion, persuasion, rejection and controversy have taken place in varying degrees. Often non-religious motives were also involved, for instance in the making of a local deity into the supreme deity of a whole area (examples of this being found in Egypt and Babylonia), where political motives were at least as important as religious ones.

Many religions, large and small, have had an intense conviction of mission, but missionary activity can be seen most clearly in the history of Buddhism, Islam and Christianity. The facts are well known in all three cases.

The study of mission as an aspect of comparative religion has, however, been strangely neglected, perhaps because of its difficulty. While it is relatively easy to evaluate a religious tradition on the basis of its own internal evidence, the problems multiply when several such traditions are involved. Not only must doctrinal matters be considered, but note must be taken of geographical, political, social and economic factors. To study the encounter of religious traditions requires knowledge of all the traditions involved. In the encounter of Christianity and Hinduism (to take only one example), the student must attempt to understand the two separately and in interaction, including the Hindu view of Christianity and the Christian view of Hinduism. The problem of conversion, its presuppositions, its conditions and its difficulties, is also involved, as is the problem of syncretism. The doctrinal basis of mission is a further factor, together with the missionary understanding of the sending agency and the establishment of religious societies among "receiving" people. Such examples of fields of study might be multiplied.

Where the serious study of mission has been undertaken, it has normally been as an aspect of Christian theology. But there is the larger area of the phenomenological study of mission waiting to be tackled. The material is there; a method can be devised; important results may be expected.

(32, 44)

26 **MYSTERY** (from Greek *mustērion*) carries in the history of religion the sense of a ritual of a private or secret nature, the character and contents of which are known (revealed) only to those who have been initiated. In the history of Christian thought, the word also has the meaning of revealed (as opposed to common) knowledge. In view of the popular use of the word as a synonym for "riddle" or "puzzle", these special meanings should be borne in mind.

The term "mystery religions" is applied to a group of cults from various parts of the world which gathered in the Hellenistic period in the Mediterranean area. Their main features were (i) the practice of initiation, by which individuals were given access to certain items of knowledge concerning a particular deity (Isis, Osiris, Demeter, Mithra, etc.) and (ii) intense concentration on the problem of life after death. The rituals of some of the mystery religions are still not known to us in detail: initiates were invariably sworn to secrecy, and the death penalty was sometimes imposed on transgressors of this vow, with the result that the secret is still in many cases inviolate. However, in other cases we are better informed. The general pattern appears to have been one of death and resurrection. The deity having died and risen again, the initiate was shown a dramatic representation of those events, and passed through certain ceremonies of assimilation to the deity, which were held to ensure safe conduct through the nether regions after death. This was the basic content of the ritual; but there were different levels of initiation, and different grades of adept.

Another common feature of the mystery religions was the sacred meal, which the initiates were believed to partake of together with the deity. The Christian Eucharist, and the practice of baptism, with certain features of early Christian terminology and belief, mean that from the technical point of view, Christianity was at first regarded as a mystery religion.

Some mystery religions occupied a favoured position in the social framework of the time. The Mysteries of Eleusis (near Athens) are a case in point. The sanctuary of Demeter at Eleusis was highly elaborate, and many prominent persons are known to have been initiates. Another mystery religion was that of Mithra (of Persian origin). Especially popular among Roman soldiers, it was thought at one time to have been a serious competitor to Christianity, though this is certainly an exaggeration. The Mysteries of Orpheus were also popular, particularly since they provided a detailed account of the topography of the nether regions, and passwords to ensure safe conduct through the land of the dead.

The reasons for the popularity of the mystery religions in Greece and Rome have been much discussed. However, it is undeniable that they gave a sense of security in face of the ultimate problem of death. Their decline was closely bound up with the rise of Christianity. In the later history of religion, cults and sects claiming to communicate hidden knowledge have flourished at certain times, particularly in periods of insecurity. Such sects may also in some cases be regarded as protests against a moribund or stagnant orthodoxy in religion.

(1, 4, 13, 14, 20, 21, 22, 34, 35, 38)

27 **MYSTICISM** is a word the implications of which are often unclear. In the study of religion it refers, however, to the immediate experience of a divine-human relationship, and in particular to the experiences of oneness with the divine. As such it is difficult to study and describe satisfactorily. Mystics tend always to claim that their experience is self-authenticating, and that it cannot be satisfactorily expressed in words. Hence there are no criteria which can be applied to mystical experience, by which the genuineness of the experience can be measured. In the last resort the student has always to treat the mystics' testimony entirely at its face value; in comparative religion the study of mysticism must remain entirely descriptive and analytical. Value-judgements can only be made on theological and metaphysical grounds.

It has sometimes been claimed that mysticism is the best possible field for work in the psychology of religion, and many psychologists have been intensely interested in the content of mystical experience. Again, however, such a study cannot venture into the area of metaphysics, where the ultimate justification of mysticism is to be found. Mystics appear on occasion to exhibit the symptoms of pathological behaviour, but this in no way invalidates (or validates) their claims to direct experience of the divine.

Mysticism is found in one form or another wherever religion is deeply felt by individuals. It is somewhat commoner in the East than in the West, but has its given place in Hinduism and Buddhism, in Judaism, Islam and Christianity. In primitive religions, the experience attributed to spirit-possession, in which the personality of the individual concerned is temporarily obliterated, has certain features in common with mysticism. Normally the essence of mystical experience is taken to be the obliteration of the distinction between subject and object, and the full identification of the worshipping subject with the object, i.e. God. This type of mysticism is most clearly seen in Hindu monism, in which the personality of the individual is lost in the infinite Brahman, or Ultimate Reality. But even in Hinduism, other schools of thought maintain that union with God does not imply the loss of individuality, and this same trend is found in Christian mysticism. Nathan Söderblom characterized the distinction between these two types as "the mysticism of the infinite" and "the mysticism of personality".

Mysticism involves a specific doctrine of God, usually what has been called the *via negativa*, which involves *inter alia* the notion that God is above and beyond all that is concrete and finite, and that his attributes can only be expressed in negatives. This is, however, not necessarily true of the mysticism of personality. It also involves intensive discipline: with few exceptions, the mystic way is recognized to be long and arduous, passing through various levels of attainment and insight to the final goal. Asceticism is a normal concomitant of mysticism: it is necessary to subdue the "flesh" in order to release the spirit for fellowship with God.

There are some forms of mysticism in which the doctrine of God and the soul are not present. The Buddhist's goal is *Nirvāna*, which is attained in ways similar to those of mysticism, but neither God nor the soul is involved.

(30, 34, 38, 42, 43)

28 **MYTH:** A myth is a type of narrative which seeks to express in imaginative form a belief about man, the world or deity which cannot adequately be expressed in simple propositions.

It is as a rule unsafe to generalize about "myth", since myths are of many types and fill many different functions in the history of religion. The student should also avoid the popular use of the word "myth" to denote untruth in general. Mythology has been used in the past as a collective noun meaning the totality of myths in a given area or tradition; its proper meaning is "the study of myths".

Ringgren has recently pointed out that two other factors are relevant to the study of myths in comparative religion. First, that a myth must be something believed and taken seriously as an explanation of an event or phenomenon. A story which is not believed in this way should be classified as legend. And secondly, that a myth should be, or have been, an element in a ritual action. It is in this context that its original meaning and function should be sought. In the course of time, many myths have become detached from their ritual framework, and it is not always possible to know what was the nature of that framework. Sometimes it may have been simple, sometimes highly elaborate, but in most cases the meaning of a myth will only be apparent when its original setting has been discovered.

Types of myths which may be mentioned as separate entities include: (a) *astral myths*, which involve beliefs in the power and influence of sun, moon and stars; (b) *nature myths*, in which natural phenomena are personified; (c) *social myths*, which account for the origin of various institutions; (d) *aitiological myths*, which explain "origins" in general.

Mythology has tended in the history of comparative religion to be an area of intensive study. Max Müller explained the origin of myths as "a disease of language", in which words for the storm, the dawn, etc., were personified because of their having gender. The anthropological school (Tylor, Lang) explained myths as primitive survivals, distinct from religion. More recently, the "myth and ritual school" has pointed out the link between myth and cult, while other scholars have concentrated on elucidating

44

the function of myth (Lévi-Strauss). Often a myth will in the course of its history have been interpreted in various ways and will have filled a variety of functions, particularly when it is incorporated into holy scripture. This makes possible a further type of historical and interpretative study; an example might be the creation narrative in the *Book of Genesis*.

It must remain an open question as to the limits of the concept of myth. To speak of Schweitzer, Churchill or Che Guevara as "a myth" implies that they have become more than historical figures, and the term may perhaps be justified. And on the psychological level, the elevation of a good story into a myth, symbolizing the conflict of good and evil and providing a focus of imaginative allegiance, is seen today in the use made in some quarters of Tolkien's *The Lord of the Rings*, and the figure of Gandalf.

Myths are clearly a primary form of religious expression, and their study along historical, psychological, sociological and other lines is more than ever necessary today.

(14, 34, 35, 40)

29 **PHENOMENOLOGY OF RELIGION:** The phenomenology of religion is a relatively new discipline within the comparative study of religion, but one which has taken its place alongside the older-established history, psychology and sociology of religion as a necessary mode of religious study. Its meaning is not, however, immediately apparent, and misunderstandings tend to arise as a result.

The term was first used by the Dutch scholar Chantepie de la Saussaye in 1887, and it has since remained the peculiar province of the Dutch. It has some affinities with the school of philosophical phenomenology, but this should not be over-stressed. The phenomenology of religion, according to C. J. Bleeker, "places

45

analogous religious phenomena . . . side by side, and tries to define their structure by comparison" (*The Sacred Bridge*, 1963, p. 2). It makes use of two important phenomenological concepts: *epoché*, the suspension of judgement as to the truth or otherwise of the phenomena studied, and the *eidetic vision*, the search for the essentials (Greek *eidos*) of religious phenomena. The phenomenologist ought, in other words, to attempt to place himself in the position of the believer, and to discern by this imaginative identification what is the essence and function of whatever it is he is studying. The phenomena studied are many of the things listed in these pages: prayer is an ideal case in point. Wherever prayer is found, it may be studied. It should be studied precisely as it is found, without manipulation and rationalization, as a mode of communication with deity. The question of the existence or otherwise of deity is left open, as is the problem of the efficacy of prayer. The student attempts by this method to discover the function of prayer in various religions, and perhaps ultimately the function of prayer as such.

It tends sometimes to be supposed that the phenomenologist has no need to be a historian. In fact the best phenomenology has been written by the best historians. The two disciplines are interdependent, at least to the extent that the history of religion (and other such disciplines) provide the data with which the phenomenologist works.

What the phenomenologist then does with his data varies from case to case. Some are content to provide a descriptive, systematic counterpart to the history of religion; others (e.g. G. van der Leeuw) go much further in their attempt to achieve an understanding of the phenomena.

The phenomenology of religion differs from the comparative religion of the earlier part of this century in that (*a*) it has abandoned the evolutionary method on which comparative religion was originally based, and which resulted in the assigning to specific religions of places on the evolutionary ladder; (*b*) it refuses altogether to attempt to compare religions as such (which was always a fruitless undertaking); and (c) it attempts to enter more fully into the inner nature of the phenomena studied, and is prepared to allow that for the purpose of understanding, "the believer is always right", while remaining completely impartial as to the final value of those phenomena. However, it should be noted, finally, that there is no final agreement among phenomenologists of religion about the precise limits of their method, and that fresh formulations of aim and scope are to be expected.

(*passim*)

30 **PRAYER** is the means by which an individual or group attempts to enter into verbal or mental communication with a deity.

Within this broad definition it is possible to distinguish many different types of prayer, including petition (popularly the dominant meaning of the word), intercession, praise and adoration. The role and the nature of prayer varies considerably from one religious tradition to another (see F. Heiler, *Prayer*, E.T., 1932), but it always presupposes belief in the existence of a supernatural world, in deity, and in the possibility of entering into contact with deity.

Prayer as a means of influencing deity was seldom found in isolation in the ancient world, usually being closely associated with ritual practices such as sacrifice. Prayer was addressed to the gods to persuade them to accept the good intention of the sacrificer, and to partake of the offerings. But just as the word of the sacrifice (*brahman* in the Indian tradition) could become in a sense more important than the sacrifice itself, so prayer could free itself from ritual action, and become not only a means of influence, but a means of communion with deity (also, of course, an aspect of sacrifice). Holy word – sacrificial formulae, the name of the deity, passages from scripture – served as an alternative channel of divine-human communication, and could be repeated in any situation. But prayer nevertheless retained its formal character.

Holy word was thus a means of mediation between man and deity. Other means were holy persons – shamans, kings, priests, devotees – whose contact with the supernatural powers was held to be direct, and who could thus communicate with the powers on behalf of common people, and holy places, in which the deity was present, and approachable. Otherwise, the need for mediation is a variable factor in prayer, and depends entirely on the underlying doctrine of God. In pantheistic religions, mediation is less necessary than in theistic religions, particularly those in which God is moral and holy. Broadly speaking, it is necessary before prayer for the worshipper to be in a state of ritual purity, to be in a "state of grace" or to have faith – all means of eliminating the gulf between man and God. The common Christian formula "through Jesus Christ our Lord" also expresses the need for mediation.

As religion becomes more intellectualized, prayer tends to lose its formal, institutional character and to become freer and more individual. There may be a reaction against formal, ritual prayer in reform movements, although this does not prevent the later formalization of "free prayer". This tendency should be distinguished from the abandonment of formal prayer in mystical movements, since in this case ritual prayer is transcended, rather than abandoned. Mental and contemplative prayer presuppose "lower" levels, and cannot be isolated from them.

Prayer as a whole requires polytheistic or theistic beliefs as a background. Non-theistic systems certainly emphasize method in relation to the Absolute, but communication in the normal sense does not take place, and prayer is replaced by meditation in the structure of religion.

(8, 19, 31, 39, 42, 50)

31 PRIEST (Priestess): A priest or priestess is a person set apart for the service of God or the gods who, by virtue of his or her office, acts as a mediator between man and deity. Normally in the history of religion priesthood has been organized into a hierarchy, headed either by the king or emperor as *pontifex maximus*, or by a high priest. The priesthood forms a special class, distinguished not only by its function but also by such outward signs as tonsure, celibacy, dress and restrictions (*tabus*) on behaviour.

The first function of a priest is to carry out ritual actions, and it is possible that priesthood originated in response to the need for persons capable of mastering increasingly complex and important rites. In this way the priest acts as a mediator between the people and their deities, between the natural and supernatural worlds. He offers sacrifice, prayer (in all its forms) and praise; he interprets oracles and the will of the gods generally; and he acts as the guardian and transmitter of holy tradition. Certain of these functions may later devolve upon other classes of persons. Often in ancient societies the roles of king and priest were virtually identical in this regard, the king being responsible for mediation on a national level, at the great shrines, while the priesthood administered the affairs of lesser and local shrines on the king's behalf. In ancient India the roles of king and priest were, however, separate: the priest (Brahmin) belonged to a higher social class than the king (a Kshatriya), and advised him in all matters belonging to religion.

While in office the priest represents the people before God or the gods; and he represents God or the gods before the people. He is set apart for this onerous duty by an act of consecration or ordination, and as a sign of his office adopts a special form of dress (during ceremonies or permanently) and special forms of behaviour. Celibacy is often, but need not always be, one such form. The priesthood may be hereditary, but in every case careful training is needed. Great emphasis may be laid on charismatic gifts, but in some societies priesthood may become little more than a department of the civil service, with appointments made on a functional and even political basis.

The progressive individualization and intellectualization of religion in the West, with correspondingly less emphasis on the need for mediation, has led to far-reaching changes in the idea of priesthood. The Christian doctrine of "the priesthood of all believers", or the direct access of the individual to God, has caused the priest to be replaced by the minister (servant of the congregation) in many branches of Christianity. An earlier example of this same development is seen in Judaism, where the destruction of the Jerusalem Temple in A.D. 70 brought to an end the sacrificial priesthood, and its replacement by the office of Rabbi (master, teacher). In other parts of the world, notably India, the function of the priest retains most of its original significance; the Brahmin is still indispensable for the correct performance of temple and household rituals in Hindu society.

It should finally be noted that, although the functions of priest and prophet have often been set up as opposites, the two were probably once closely related: a priest could well be a prophet (interpreter of the will of God) and vice versa.

(5, 8, 20, 32, 37, 39, 41, 45)

32 **PROPHET** (Prophecy): A prophet, although generally taken to be a foreteller of the future, is in comparative religion a forth-teller (Greek *prophētēs*), of the will of God or the gods. Where a religious tradition involves a distinctive view of time and eschatology, the foretelling of the future may well be part of the work of the prophet, but in general he is a mediator of divine revelation concerning past, present and future alike.

Basic to a belief in prophecy is belief in the possibility of contact with the spirit-world, particularly through gifted individuals or shamans. Spirit-possession (the literal meaning of "inspiration") was one means of contact; in such a state, often involving ecstasy, the will and intentions of the spirits were made known and communicated. The cult-centre and its rituals often included an establishment of servants of the gods who interpreted the divine will to the people. Such interpretation involved a variety of techniques – mechanical divination, ecstatic experiences, dreams, visions, auditions. As mediation between the natural and supernatural worlds, this may be regarded as priesthood; as communication, it may equally be regarded as prophecy, and the relationship between the two is often indistinct. Great cult-centres had "schools" of prophets or seers, who were resorted to by kings and others when a particular course of action needed to be justified or evaluated.

Thus while one type of prophecy took place generally on an *ad hoc* basis, the contribution of individual prophets might have more universal significance, particularly in writing cultures, where prophecy could be preserved and accorded normative significance as holy writ. The oracles of the later prophets of Israel became part of the Bible as a counterpart to the law and the writings; the oracles communicated to Muhammad became the Qur'an. In each case the prophecy in its written form, since it was given by God to a peculiarly receptive individual, could still be regarded as divine revelation.

There is always the possibility of conflict between rival prophets or schools of prophecy, either because of different underlying views of the divine nature and will, or because prophets may be speaking for different deities. Several such conflicts are recorded in the Old Testament, e.g. in 1 Kgs. 18 and 22, while the term "false prophecy" implies the communication of the will of a deity or spirit other than the true God.

The greatest prophets called for individual commitment, and often opposed stereotyped religious forms. Partly because of this, there has been a tendency in recent scholarship to over-emphasize the isolation of the prophet from the religious traditions of his time. As a rule the prophet was a radical in the original sense of the word, calling for a return to the root, *radix*, of his tradition. In so doing he would often gather a company of disciples, and might deliberately or accidentally start a new religious tradition or a sect. There has never been a total religious innovator: prophetic religion is a combination of renewal, heresy and innovation; however, because of the strength of its personal conviction and the direct revelation to which it appeals, it usually has greater strength and resilience than the institutional religion out of which it has emerged.

(5, 8, 9, 19, 25, 38, 40, 47)

33 **RELIGION:** Definitions of religion are legion, depending in the last resort on the presuppositions of the student, and it is doubtful whether any short definition can do justice to the essential complexity of the subject. Religion clearly contains intellectual, ritual, social and ethical elements, bound together by an explicit or implicit belief in the reality of an unseen world, whether this belief be expressed in supernaturalistic or idealistic terms. In the history of comparative religion there has been a common tendency to isolate one or other of these elements as "original" or "central", with consequent neglect of others. The result has in many cases been serious distortion.

Etymological definitions are of little value: Cicero, *De Natura Deorum*, derived "religion" from *relegere* (to re-read or reflect); Lactantius, *Divinarum Institutionum Libri VII*, from *religare* (to bind fast).

Modern definitions tend to approach the subject either from the individual or the social angle. Among individualist definitions are those of Schleiermacher ("the feeling of absolute dependence"), Whitehead ("force of belief cleansing the inward parts . . . the art and the theory of the internal life of man . . . what the individual does with his own solitariness"), Menzies ("the worship of higher powers from a sense of need"). Among social definitions, the best known is that of Durkheim, who called religion "an eminently collective thing", and defined a religion as "a unified system of beliefs and practices relative to sacred things". A widely accepted compromise definition is that of J. B. Pratt: "Religion is the serious and social attitude of individuals or communities toward the power or powers which they conceive as having ultimate control over their interests and destinies" (*The Religious Consciousness*, 1921, p. 2).

The study of religion in its full complexity can now only be carried out by means of dividing the field, recognizing that no one method or approach can do justice to all its manifestations. The constituent disciplines of comparative religion are: 1. The history of religion, in which separate religious traditions are dealt with by strict historical method. 2. The sociology of religion, which concentrates on the collective forms of religion. 3. The psychology of religion, in which the beliefs of individuals are considered. 4. The phenomenology of religion, which systematizes religious phenomena on the basis of the data provided by 1, 2 and 3. Philosophy, philology, geography, archaeology, anthropology, etc., may be regarded as "auxiliary sciences". It should be recognized that the old ideal of comparing religions as totalities has now for the most part been abandoned, and that there is no longer any question of assigning religions places on an evolutionary ladder, or relative value as types.

If religion be regarded as a mode of human behaviour, having reference to ultimate values and to the quest for permanence and reality, then certain ideologies may be studied on essentially the same terms as religion. It is, however, inadvisable to speak of pseudo-religions in this context, owing to the difficulty of finding suitable criteria for separating "genuine" from "pseudo-" religions. In every case the student should suspend judgement as to the ultimate value of the material studied: to make judgements of value is to enter the field of theology, in which different (though entirely proper) methods are necessary.

(passim)

34 **REVELATION,** from Latin *revelatio*, is the showing to man by deity of things otherwise hidden from him. Theories and doctrines of revelation centre on the means by which deity communicates these things to man, and the means by which man is enabled to receive them.

In archaic religions, revelation depends on the presence within the tribe of people or individuals capable of making contact with the spirit-world. What is communicated in these cases is first of all supernatural power, and secondly the knowledge by which that power may be controlled and exercised. Shamanism, and divinatory practices generally, may be said to contain a rudimentary view of revelation. In the ancient civilizations of the Near East and elsewhere, the king received divine knowledge by means of dreams, visions, the interpretation of omens and, as writing developed, codes of law. In all these cases, revelation was something to be received by a peculiarly gifted individual, and then passed on to the people as a whole.

Although revelation was thus originally passed on orally, from the fourth millennium B.C. it came to be codified and transmitted in the form of holy (i.e. revealed) scripture, containing accounts of the activity of God or the gods, laws for the regulation of human life according to the divine will, and ritual injunctions. The authority of revelation in such cases was derived from the situation in which it had been originally communicated, and the person through whom deity had spoken. The Sanskrit word for revelation is *shruti*, "that which has been heard", i.e. by the ancient wise men (*rishis*). Behind the Old Testament stands the figure of Moses, behind the Qur'an the person of Muhammad, behind the New Testament the figures of Jesus and the first apostles, and so on.

Although oral and written revelation of specific divine injunctions has been normative in most religions, other forms have not been ruled out, since deity is clearly free to continue to communicate with man. And as times change, and the need for further interpretation of scripture grows, supplementary revelations occur. The prophet may challenge tradition on the basis of a "new" revelation, as may the reformer. The individual may claim direct insight into the divine nature and will, or assert that the truth of divine revelation is beyond all conceptual formulation. Revelation may in these situations become a matter of pure intuition, and conflicts with religious authority may be created.

In the recent history of religion in the West, the doctrine of revelation has been a matter of much debate. Not only has the doctrine of God changed in the direction of immanentism – bringing about a devaluation of the idea of the communication of "truths" from some external supernatural source – but man's capacity for receiving such revelation has been called in question. The idea of revelation rests in every case on a prior conception of the nature of deity, and cannot be understood apart from the theology which underlies it.

(8, 9, 18, 19, 26, 27, 31, 32, 40)

35 **RITUAL,** from Latin *ritus* ("sacred custom"), denotes any form of behaviour the characteristics of which are fixed by tradition. In the study of religion it means "traditional religious behaviour or actions", in which sense it is close in meaning to "cult" (Lat. *cultus*, "worship").

The ritual element in religion cannot easily be separated from the element of faith and belief. The fact that certain rituals are regularly performed implies certain underlying beliefs, but it is not possible to conclude that belief is therefore prior to, or more important than, ritual. In the history of religion ritual and belief have been intimately connected, and as a rule a belief has become effective only when acted out. It is, however, possible for a ritual to survive when its original justification has been forgotten, or to take on new dimensions of meaning in the course of history. New rituals are constantly being created, sometimes with explicit religious content, sometimes not. Psychologically these may serve to identify and establish a group or party (as in the case of mass demonstrations), but a more basic function is that of imposing order on an otherwise haphazard world.

Religious ritual presupposes the existence of a supernatural or divine order, revealed in what are to us natural occurrences such as the alternation of life and death, day and night, the movements of heavenly bodies and the progression of the seasons. It was further believed that the continuation of that order would be ensured only if man remained in right relation to the supernatural powers, and one elementary function of ritual was to maintain the divine-human relationship by means of seasonal and daily celebrations. These celebrations, and particularly those in spring or at the new year, involved the recitation of the deeds of the gods in creation and the symbolical re-creation of the world. Ritual and myth were thus closely linked. Also involved were the physical actions – dancing, music and drama – in which the divine acts were symbolically repeated and renewed. In its religious aspect, ritual is essentially drama – a drama in which the whole of man is involved.

Rituals are, of course, of many types, but common to them all is the conviction that what is being done approximates to the divine order as supernaturally revealed. The nature of the divine order may be understood in different ways: it may be highly

56

mythologized or almost entirely inward, intellectual and spiritual. But it would be wrong to interpret the reactions of one religious group against the ritual expressions of another (a common feature in religious reformation) as implying a total rejection of ritual. A Catholic High Mass is one form of ritual; a Quaker meeting is another. Each corresponds to, and cannot be understood apart from, a body of convictions concerning God and man, and the relationship between the two.

The student of comparative religion should be aware that religion is something involving the whole man, and that to concentrate on beliefs and philosophies is to study only part of religion. The study of ritual, and its means of expression in art, music and drama, has been seriously neglected by scholarship for far too long, with a consequent distortion of perspective. This whole area needs to be considered afresh, not least in the context of the so-called secularization of religion.

(7, 14, 28, 50)

36 **SACRED** (Holy): Sacred (from Lat. *sacer*) and holy (from OE *halig*, cf. German *heilig*) are synonyms for that which belongs to the sphere of deity and the supernatural, as opposed to the profane or the secular, which belongs to the common order of things. Both are adjectives qualifying persons, places or objects in which the supernatural world interpenetrates with the everyday world. It is possible to use them in a substantive sense ("the sacred", cf. Otto's book *Das Heilige*, E. T. *The Idea of the Holy*), but this may give rise to misunderstandings. One such has been the attempt to explain the origin of all religion in the "sense of the holy" experienced by primitive man in his encounters with the unknown and the inexplicable. The main fault of this view is that it places the emphasis on the nature of man's experience – an area in which precise information is practically unobtainable.

Leaving aside the question of origins, the evidence shows that for the greater part of his history, man has believed in the actual existence of a world parallel to his own, a world made up of unseen beings ranging from the high gods of the sky (who may often be remote) down through lesser deities, emanations, angels, spirits and demons to the ghosts of the departed. Wherever, and in whatever way, this parallel world meets man's normal world, it is appropriate to speak of the point of contact as being "sacred". The sacrificial site, temple, or church is a sacred place; the king or priest is a sacred person; the book in which the deity reveals his will is a sacred scripture; the dance, music, song and speech in which the supernaturals are celebrated is a sacred ritual; and so on.

The sacred person, object or place must always be treated with the utmost care, and can only be approached after rites of purification. In the absence of such preparation, the sacred may be thoroughly dangerous (not unlike electricity); if not directly dangerous, the efficacy of a ritual may be nullified if it should be approached carelessly. Hunting rituals provide a case in point. The hunter, before setting out on an expedition, had to observe continence, sexual and other, since to approach the supernatural owners of the animals without such precautions would inevitably mean failure.

The twentieth century has seen the erosion of belief in the supernatural within many religions, particularly Christianity, but also in e.g. sections of Judaism and Hinduism. This process of secularization makes it hard for the modern student of comparative religion to take seriously the beliefs held in the past concerning the supernatural. It should be emphasized, however, that the student must attempt to understand the sacred as far as possible as archaic man understood it. The assigning by sociologists and others of unconscious motives to religions of the past is of strictly limited value. Söderblom's words: "Real religion may exist without a definite conception of divinity, but there is no real religion without a distinction between holy and profane", and his definition of religion as: "Religious is the man to whom something is holy" (*ERE*, VI, 731), contain a large measure of truth.

(*passim*)

37 **SACRIFICE** is the act of dedicating a person, an animal or an object to a deity, either in order to influence the deity in some way or in order to create a bond of fellowship between the deity and the worshipper. There are, within this definition, various types of sacrifice, according to the motive which predominates. The simplest motive is that of devotion, coupled with the desire to give gifts to the gods, and the conviction that the gods were in some way nourished by the things – and particularly the food – sacrificed to them. To fail to sacrifice would therefore tend either to weaken the gods, or to arouse their ill-will.

A well-known example of this is found in the Babylonian *Epic of Gilgamesh*, in which the great flood deprives the gods of sacrificial food; when the flood subsides, and sacrifice is once more offered by the survivors, the gods gather round "like flies". As with the gods, so with the departed spirits, who are nourished by sacrifices made at the grave or in their former home. In the Hindu *Bhagavad Gita*, if the "fathers" are deprived of sacrificial food, they are said to be in danger of falling down from heaven. Sacrifice in this sense may be made by libation and grave-offerings (where the dead live on in or near the tomb), or by fire (where the dead live with the gods in the celestial regions). In each case what is consumed is the spiritual essence of the food.

Sacrifice may further be made as a means of atonement, i.e. as a means of transferring the sins of individuals or groups to (usually) animals who are then delivered into the power of deities or spirits. Many of the sacrifices in the Old Testament are of this type. The "scapegoat" was driven into the desert, bearing the sins of the people, to be a sacrifice to a spirit, Azazel (Lev. 16:10), but most sacrificial animals were killed and burned on the altar. The Christian doctrine of the sacrifice of Christ goes back to these ideas. (cf. Heb. 9:12).

Thirdly, sacrifice may have the aspect of communion. Deity and worshippers may share a common meal (as worshippers are offered the sacrificial food and drink). This is a common practice in many religions – one example among many being the Hindu practice of offering the worshipper *prasada* (food) and *tirtha* (drink) from the deity's table. The Jewish Passover, at which the sacrificial lamb was killed, offered and eaten, is another such example, recalled by Paul: '... are not those who eat the sacrifices partners in the altar?' (1 Cor. 10:18). The table-fellowship with the deity may also anticipate the eschatological banquet – as in the Christian Eucharist.

Sacrificial practices lend themselves to spiritualization and allegory, and in modern times it is common to find records referring to sacrifice interpreted on a basis of the individual's relationship to God, and not literally.

(1, 2, 5, 13, 23, 31, 35, 39, 42, 45, 50)

38 **SALVATION (SAVIOUR):** The idea that man needs to be delivered, by divine agency, from ills, imperfections and misfortunes is a common one in most forms of religion. Soteriologies (from Greek *sōtēr*, saviour, *sōtēria*, salvation) are nevertheless of many different kinds, depending on (*a*) the nature of the ill from which man is to be delivered, (*b*) the state into which he is then passed, and (*c*) the nature of the saviour god.

Early ideas of salvation see man's state as essentially one of powerlessness; in contrast to the gods he is mortal, liable to disease and death. Although these may be believed to be caused by the agency of malevolent spirits (as in most primitive religions), salvation may in such cases mean little more than the gift of a long and healthy life, and the enjoyment of material benefits. Germanic words for "health", "wholeness" and "salvation" are closely related. The achievement of immortality clearly could not take place in the world, because the gods were not willing – a point of view expressed frequently in Mesopotamian religion. But there was always the possibility of the achievement of immortality beyond death, and other soteriologies concentrate on this aspect. Man is thus saved from final annihilation, as in Egyptian religion and the Greek mysteries. Where the world is believed to be under the control of evil spirits, salvation means deliverance from their power, and man's establishment under the will of a benevolent deity; this aspect was prominent in early and medieval Christianity. It was, however, linked with another idea, that of man's deliverance from his own evil nature, i.e. from the guilt and power of sin. Since evil brought its own punishment, meted out by a holy and righteous God, salvation could involve the avoidance of punishment and the achievement of final blessedness, though the gift of fellowship with God was of more importance. And finally, in Eastern religions, salvation is understood as meaning release from the round of rebirth; since rebirth is conditioned by ignorance and desire, salvation is usually (though not always) seen as the attainment of knowledge. In this case the word "salvation" is misleading; "release" is better.

The means by which salvation is brought about by the saviour god (or goddess) also vary. In Christianity the idea of incarnation is prominent, as it is in some forms of Hindu thought; God becomes man in order to deliver him from evil. In the mystery religions, salvation was brought about by ritual assimilation to a god who was believed to have died and risen again from the dead, or who had intimate knowledge of the world of the dead (Isis, Osiris, Demeter, Orpheus, etc.). In Islam, salvation is by an act of

61

simple obedience to the revealed will of God. Hindu saviour gods (e.g. Krishna, Rama, Shiva) call forth the devotion (*bhakti*) of the worshipper, freeing his soul from its bondage to the material world.

There are apparent soteriologies in which the idea of divine agency is not present: in early and Theravada Buddhism, man could be saved only through his own efforts, and no deity was involved; however, Mahayana Buddhism made the Buddha into a saviour, and introduced the doctrine of "saints" (*bodhisattvas*) as supernatural helpers.

The whole subject of soteriology is one of extreme complexity, involving distinctive views of deity, of the nature of man, of time and of the world. Clearly there is no universal soteriology, and efforts to reconcile conflicting views of religion often do so by ignoring the problem of man's salvation altogether.

(11, 17, 19, 20, 21, 22, 26, 42, 43)

39 **SANCTUARY:** A sanctuary is in religious belief a holy place, a meeting place of man and God. The word is derived from Latin *sanctuarium*; a parallel Latin word is *fanum*, whence our word "profane", *profanus* (outside the sphere of the sacred).

In the history of religion there are many examples of such holy places, beginning with mountains and caves, where deity was believed to be present in an especially high degree. There rituals were carried out to ensure the benevolence of deity and to preserve the natural order. The earliest known temples preserved, whether by accident or design, much of the mountain and cave symbolism. The temple might be built on a hilltop, or on an artificial hill, as in Mesopotamia; it might represent the mountain-home of the gods, as in India; and the innermost room of the temple, in which the deity had his or her home, was like a cave in having no window and often only a small entrance.

The temple was the place where the deity had condescended to live and to manifest himself to men: thus it may be described as *domus dei*, the house of God. In this type of sanctuary, particularly the more elaborate examples, there was a close parallel to the royal court, with the "king's" chamber approached through outer chambers. Only the high priest, or the king, could enter the "holy of holies", though the deity was served by an entire household. Worshippers were not as a rule permitted to enter the inner courts, although they might be allowed to look into the central shrine on special occasions.

The other major type of sanctuary is the *domus ecclesiae*, the house of the congregation, typified by the Jewish synagogue, the Muslim mosque and certain types of Christian church. Here the house is made holy not by the presence of an image of God, but by a symbol of God in word (the Torah, Qur'an, Bible) and sacrament, or by the presence of the worshipping congregation. In some parts of the world (e.g. America) the word "sanctuary" is reserved for that part of a complex of buildings in which worship takes place.

Although the *domus ecclesiae* does not require the elaborate ceremonial of the *domus dei*, there are special modes of behaviour appropriate to it. These often involve conventions of dress (the wearing of hats and shoes), and vary greatly between traditions.

Since the deity is the guardian of law and justice, and since life (symbolized in many traditions by blood) is particularly sacred to the deity, no shedding of blood might take place in the sanctuary other than that offered directly in sacrifice to the deity. Hence the derived meaning of "sanctuary" as a place of safety, a place where the fugitive, whatever his crime, might enjoy the protection of the deity.

The idea of the qualitative distinction between a sanctuary and the world outside requires that a prior distinction be made between sacred (that belonging to the sphere of the supernatural) and the profane. In recent years this distinction has become blurred, particularly in the West, with the result that a building used for worship can now be put to virtually any other use – an unthinkable step for anyone to whom the sanctuary is a genuine focus of holiness.

(5, 8, 9, 14, 18, 31, 45, 50)

40 **SCRIPTURE:** The student of comparative religion has frequent occasion to refer to the scriptures of the great religions and their lesser offshoots. Normally the study of languages is the needle's eye through which the student must pass in order to gain close first-hand knowledge of such sources. Translations are not always reliable, and may sometimes be very unreliable indeed. However, a study of religion which bases itself only on the philological study of scripture is inadequate. It is necessary to know how the canon (rule, norm) of scripture in a given area has been created, and why some "holy scriptures" are more holy than others. Hindu scripture, for instance, is divided into the categories of *shruti* (revelation) and *smriti* (tradition), which are used in different ways by Hindus. The Jewish division of scripture into written and oral *Torah* (law) is a further case in point, while the understanding of Christianity by means of the writings of fathers, commentators, reformers, etc., is a necessary complement to a purely biblical understanding.

For a full understanding of a religious tradition, it is necessary to view holy scripture in the light of the totality of that tradition. It is, of course, important to know what a written source meant to the writer, and what was the precise message which it was originally intended to convey, but it is equally important to study traditions of scriptural interpretation. So while on the one hand the student will ideally use all the tools of Western scholarship to establish original texts and to collate variant readings, he must on

64

the other hand attempt to read with the eye of the faithful, and to treat, say, the *Bhagavad Gita*, the *Qur'an* or the *Gospel of John* as representing divine revelation. And since virtually all scripture is understood in revelatory terms – culminating in the reverence accorded by Sikhs to the *Guru Granth Sahib* – there must be some prior understanding of Hindu, Jewish, Christian, Muslim and other doctrines of God and doctrines of revelation.

It is also important to study the use of scripture – as a source of information about sacred history, as a collection of edifying stories for the faithful to imitate, as matter for meditation, leading to direct knowledge of God, and so on. The sectarian use of Scripture is a further area of specialist study. The Christian Scientist, for example, views the Old Testament through the prism of the New, and reads both in the light of *Science and Health*. Many other such examples might be given.

The changing role of scripture in the major religious traditions is a good guide to the development of those traditions whether the examples chosen be the liberal-fundamentalist controversy in Christianity, the notion of Vedic authority in Hinduism, or some other. But in every case, linguistic study must be backed up by inquiry into background and social setting, if a total view is to be obtained. Few individual students may be in a position to gain such an overall view, but it is well to bear the ideal in mind.

(5, 8, 19, 28, 34, 36)

41 **SHAMAN (SHAMANISM)**: The word "shaman" is of northern Asiatic origin, and means "priest" or "medicine man".

Shamanism is properly used to describe the indigenous religion of northern Eurasia, but is often taken to refer to a type of primitive religion in which certain features, notably trance and the control of spirits, are prominent.

Shamanism is always found among hunting peoples, and always presupposes a belief in "animism", i.e. a multiplicity of spirits, and in the continued existence of the soul after death. Shamans may inherit their office, but in every case have to undergo a period of intensive training in order to fit them for their role as mediators between the world of men and the world of the spirits. The shaman may be an epileptic, or otherwise liable to fits and trances; in his training he is subjected to severe ascetic disciplines, which are believed to bestow upon him supernatural powers, and to establish contact between him and his familiar spirits. An elaborate rite of initiation is carried out, in which he is given authority and control over these spirits, and he is then invested with a special dress and special equipment. The most important single item of equipment is the drum, which is ornamented with symbolical signs and figures (the best-known examples of this are from Lapland), and by which he is able to call and gather the spirits.

The shaman is a priest, in that he carries out mediatorial functions on behalf of his people. He offers sacrifices, interprets the will of the gods and spirits, and cures (or attempts to cure) diseases. Since it is believed in many primitive societies that disease is caused by the loss of the individual's free-soul, the shaman attempts to pursue the spirits which have stolen it, to overcome them and to return the soul to its owner – all in a state of trance. Thus it is taken for granted that the shaman is able to project his own soul into the spirit-world, and there to engage in combat (or persuasion) with harmful beings. The Eskimo shaman, for instance, will "visit" the undersea abode of the goddess Sedna in order to attempt to persuade her to release seals and walruses for man's food.

When undertaking a "spirit-flight", the shaman had a special tent made for him, the centre-pole of which represented the cosmic tree. He went into a trance, partly by self-hypnosis, in which singing and the beating of the drum played a part. This trance might communicate itself to some of his watchers. During or after the "flight" he would describe to the people his experiences. In some cases he would not undertake the "flight" himself, but would have an animal double to act on his behalf.

Shamanism as a coherent world-view is now practically extinct, but certain broadly shamanistic practices survive in various parts of the world – the practices of so-called "witch doctors" being a case in point.

(2, 5, 8, 9, 13, 20, 23, 31, 36, 43, 49)

42 **SIN** tends to be understood in the West exclusively in the sense of the transgression of divine commandments, but in comparative religion it has a much wider meaning, viz., any departure from a divinely instituted order. Sin can only be moral if and when the underlying conception of God is also moral, and in many early ideas of sin the ritual element is more prominent than the ethical element.

The cosmic order established by deity is characterized by balance, harmony and regularity, and man can contribute to its maintenance by his own faithfulness in the performance of sacrifice, and his own acceptance of his relationship to deity. It also has a social dimension, in that relationships between men are similarly regulated. Thus the earliest confessions of sin which we possess (from ancient Egypt and Mesopotamia) include the confession of ritual, legal and moral transgressions almost indiscriminately. To fail to sacrifice, to use false measures and to steal or murder were all transgressions against the order called in Egypt *ma'at*. Similar confessions are found in early Vedic hymns to the god Varuna as the guardian of order (*rita*), while the laws of the Old Testament contain ritual, ethical and legal

67

injunctions, all of which were regarded as the will of God for his people.

Sin is always punishable, either by the simple withdrawal of the favour of deity, by death, or by more protracted punishments in the life to come. But except in the gravest cases, the sin might be wiped out by an act of atonement, usually involving sacrifice. Sin might be accidental; the state of ritual purity could be spoiled by accidental contact with blood, a corpse, or an unclean person or animal; all this was in effect sin, and required an act of purification.

Central to Christianity is the idea that man is incapable of making atonement for sin (thought of in moral terms), since a transgression against infinite holiness must *ipso facto* be infinite. Thus atonement can be made only by Christ, and man can only receive forgiveness. Original sin, in the Christian view, is an innate tendency to act in ways unacceptable to God. Few other religions have such a concept, though in Indian religions generally man, since he is born in human form, is imprisoned in the fetters of matter, from which he must be freed either through the attainment of knowledge or through the grace of God. Sin in this context is ignorance, and may have little moral content.

A common feature of many religions is the tendency to classify sin in categories, according to the punishment they merit, and the measures required for their expiation. In classical Hindu belief the killing of a Brahmin is one of the gravest of all sins, while the killing of a cow is more serious than the murder of an outcaste. In Catholic Christianity sins are divided into mortal sins, meriting eternal punishment, and venial sins, which do not separate the believer from God.

However, sin always involves separation from God, a separation which may be temporary or permanent; and to understand the concept of sin in any religion it is necessary first of all to understand the underlying doctrine of God.

(11, 19, 26, 31, 35, 36, 37)

43 SOUL, SPIRIT: According to the theory of animism, early man was led by his experiences in dream and trance to the belief in a separable, non-material soul or spirit, distinct from the body. This is of course conjecture, but it is certain that primitive peoples have such beliefs, and that they are most clearly expressed in connection with dream, trance or death. These beliefs are, however, seldom logical or consistent, and it may seem that primitive races believe in a plurality of souls. One has been called the "free-soul", which leaves the body in sleep or trance, and which is regarded as the source of consciousness; another the "life-soul", expressing physical or psychical activity, and the source of human life. In some quarters the soul might be held to be pre-existent or subject to rebirth in a series of bodies. Old age, disease and death were all held to be signs of the loss of the free-soul. The agency in such cases might be an evil spirit or the activities of a shaman; having once left the body, it might return only if it did not stray too near the land of the dead. On death, the free-soul left the body first, followed by the life-soul. After death, the various souls might suffer various fates, becoming ghosts, going to the land of the dead or being reborn.

It is usual in religious belief to assume that the body and the soul are distinct, and that the soul is only a temporary inhabitant of the body. Indeed, the body may be believed to imprison the soul, which is of the essence of divinity, and is constantly bound to seek to return to its proper sphere – an assumption which underlies virtually the whole of the Indian religious tradition, and is also found in ancient Greece, whence we have the celebrated formula *sōma-sēma*, "the body a tomb", i.e. of the soul. In India, the soul, *ātman*, finds salvation on being liberated from the body and merged into the ultimate Reality, *brahman*. In the Gnostic tradition the soul, *pneuma*, is an emanation of the divine, with which it strives to be reunited.

A rather special case is provided by Theravada Buddhism, which holds to the non-existence of the soul (the doctrine of *anattā*), claiming that what is popularly supposed to be a soul, spirit or essential Self is no more than a temporary agglomeration of constituent factors (*khandhas*).

The Semitic tradition, from which the Judaeo-Christian tradition is derived, also has a distinctive view, maintaining that soul and body are intimately connected, and that human personality relates to both. However, in the Old Testament and more especially in the New Testament there is an elaborate doctrine of the soul, or spirit, worked out partly in contrast to the qualities of the body and the flesh. Thus although the New Testament emphasizes the unity of soul and body, popular Christian belief has always tended to separate them, and to assume – in line with popular religious belief in all ages – that it is the non-material part of man which stands in relationship to God, and which survives death.

The continued existence of souls after death, and the independent existence of spirits as an intermediate order of being between deity and man, has given rise to a large variety of beliefs and rites – ancestor worship, propitiatory rites and what is commonly called "spiritualism", i.e. the belief that the souls of the dead can be contacted, and can be communicated with. Practices of this order have often been regarded with disfavour by religious authorities.

(2, 9, 22, 32, 41)

44 **SYNCRETISM** is a word derived from the Greek *synkretizein*, "to hold together like Cretans"; it denotes any form of religion in which elements from more than one original religious tradition are combined. It was first used by Plutarch in the neutral sense of "reconciliation", and in the sixteenth century was still being used in the same way to refer to those who wished to reconcile extreme positions. In the history of Christian thought, therefore, it has had a meaning not far removed from "liberalism". Only in the recent history of comparative religion has it been

used in a more technical sense, first to refer to these religions of the Greco-Roman period in which deities and practices from various parts of the world were freely combined, and then to refer to any such mingling of religious elements.

The word has, however, very frequently had pejorative overtones, particularly when used by the adherents of an orthodox form of religion to refer to the less orthodox. It was often used in Christian missionary literature to criticize (or at least warn against) the importation of "foreign" elements into Christianity. And it is generally true to say that to speak of syncretism presupposes an orthodox form of religion with which external elements have been combined. Thus syncretism in the religion of Israel implies a more or less corrupt form of popular religion, under the influence of e.g. the Canaanite cults.

The accuracy of the term in comparative religion depends to a great extent on the degree to which "religions" are regarded as having a normal, ideal form and content. This is more likely to be a theological than a historical or phenomenological judgement. From the descriptive point of view, the history of any major religious tradition consists of a constant process of adaptation to new and changing environments and to the encounter with other traditions. No religious tradition is monolithic, fixed once and for all in every detail; tradition is cumulative, and is bound in the natural course of events to be in constant receipt of influences from the religious and secular environment. The adoption of elements of belief and practice from another tradition may be deliberate, as part of a conscious attempt at adaptation; but more often it is entirely unconscious. The Christian adoption of the date of the festival of *sol invictus* as Christmas Day was deliberate; the Christianization of pre-Christian elements in the festival was an unconscious process.

Probably, therefore, it would be wiser to speak of syncretism only in those cases where a deliberate fusion of material from differing traditions takes place. In all other cases the process should be regarded as part of the normal development of a tradition. Whether the term should still be used in a theological sense to denote a departure from an accepted norm is a matter which it is outside our scope to discuss.

(25, 29)

45 **TABU** (or Taboo) is a word of Polynesian origin which has come to be used in comparative religion to denote anything or anyone set apart, consecrated, and therefore "out of bounds" to ordinary people. It is closely related as a technical term to *mana* (q.v.), and is subject to the same potential misunderstanding: its area of reference is to that which is the property of the spirit-world, and there is nothing of "impersonal power" involved in it. Broadly speaking, then, a person, place or object in which the spirit-world impinges upon the normal world has the quality of *mana*, and is subject to *tabu*.

The supernatural power which the spirits control is considered in primitive belief to be communicable to persons, especially kings, chiefs and priests, who are dedicated to the spirits or gods. Such persons are mediators between men and gods, guardians on behalf of their people of the divine order, and possessors of more than normal power. In their own persons they were *tabu*, and might not be approached directly or touched by the common people. Their power (*mana*) was communicable, and they were able to place a *tabu* on a person, a hut or an object. Similarly a cult-centre was *tabu* because of being the place in which the spirits communicated with men; cult-objects – images, instruments, symbols – were *tabu* likewise. The conditions on which an approach might be made were identical in principle, although variable in practice: purification rites, aimed at removing every trace of possible ritual pollution.

The source of pollution might well involve another type of *tabu*, viz., that in which the individual had come into contact with blood, with a corpse or with a particular animal or bird. These, too, were *tabu* because of being peculiarly the property of deity or the spirits, and where inadvertent contact had taken place, it was necessary to restore the *status quo* by means of appropriate rituals, usually involving sacrifice.

In general it is true to say that anything which is held to be sacred may be subject to some form of restriction of access, or at least to restrictions of behaviour corresponding in intention, if not in intensity, to *tabu*. There is in effect a *tabu* on Mecca which prevents any but Muslims entering the holy place; the *Veda* (the holy scriptures of Brahmanical Hinduism) have been communicated to non-Brahmins only in very recent times; the content of the Hellenistic mystery religions was a closely guarded secret, and access to the shrines was restricted to initiates. Thus *tabu* in its broadest sense is lifted in many cases on condition of initiation, or membership of an appropriate group – a phenomenon corresponding to the condition of ritual purity in primitive belief.

Clearly there is a sociological dimension to belief in *tabu*, since a sacred object, person or place has to be held sacred by the group, and not merely by an individual; but the belief as such cannot be explained solely on sociological grounds. As in so many other cases, it depends in the last resort on beliefs in the existence of a supernatural world, and where such belief is relaxed or attenuated, *tabu* is unlikely to be enforced.

(2, 24, 36, 39, 42)

46 **THEISM (AND DERIVATIVES):** One of the more regrettable tendencies of Western thought since the eighteenth century has been its delight in "-isms". To speak of a religion or a school of thought or practice as an "-ism" is dangerous in

that it encourages the idea that everything apparently within it conforms to a given pattern – which is seldom or never the case. But the verbal habit is by now a deep-rooted one, and this being so, there are a number of "-isms" in comparative religion which require attention.

We cannot in this context enter into a discussion of words like Hinduism, Buddhism, Judaism, Gnosticism and Methodism, each of which denotes, or appears to denote, a distinct area of religion, and which may continue to serve, provided the need for further definition and greater precision is borne in mind. But there are a number of more general words having to do with the central area of belief in God, *theos*, as follows:

1. *Theism*. The doctrine that there is one supreme Reality which is both morally perfect and therefore also an adequate object of adoration and worship. On this view, the deity is personal in the sense of being willing to enter into a relationship with man.

2. *Deism* (from Latin *deus*, God). A view common in the West in the eighteenth century, in which God, although perfect and moral, is remote from man and does not desire communication with him.

3. *Atheism*. The denial of the existence of a personal, moral, Supreme Being. In the West the word is often synonymous with "materialism", and implies the denial of the existence of anything but matter; in some Eastern traditions (e.g. Buddhism), the existence of a creative Supreme Being is denied, but not the existence of spiritual beings.

4. *Polytheism*. The belief in many deities.

5. *Henotheism*. A word coined by Friedrich Max Müller to denote the belief in many deities, but the worship of only one deity. The tendency to see separate deities as functions or aspects of one great deity may be described by this term.

6. *Monotheism*. The belief in one God.

7. *Pantheism*. A word used to denote the belief that God is present in all things, and that all things serve to reveal God

(natural revelation). This view is particularly common in the Indian religious tradition, although in many cases linked with the idea that the supreme *brahman* (Reality) is ultimately other than the material world. In this tradition it is also proper to speak of *ontological monism*, i.e. the belief that all reality is one.

5. *Panentheism*. The belief that although all things are in God, the nature of God is not exhausted by these manifestations. God is greater than the sum of the ways in which he reveals himself, being both immanent and transcendent. This is a fairly common view in the history of religion, although the word itself is relatively uncommon.

47 **TIME:** The awareness of the passage of time is a basic condition of all human thought, and the categories of past, present and future are of vital importance in all religion. It has in fact been maintained that religion originated from man's sense of insecurity in face of the passage of time (see S. G. F. Brandon, *Time and Mankind*, 1951, *History, Time and Deity*, 1965). In common with all theories of the origin of religion, this is incapable of either proof or disproof, but it is certain that the religions of mankind attempt in various ways to come to terms with time.

A basic proposition in the religious view of time is that man is bound by the limitations of earthly existence: he is born, he grows old and dies, and he is able to predict this course of events. But he is also able to envisage an ideal order in which such limitations do not apply – a spirit-world free from the bonds of time and space. Certain types of experience, and especially those associated with sleep, dream and trance, intoxication and ecstasy, are interpreted as being a breaking free from human limitations and a sharing of the timelessness (immortality) of the spirits and gods.

To achieve contact by ritual means with the spirit-world is therefore to ensure the immortality of man, or some part of man. This part is generally speaking not the body, but the soul, which is in any case usually regarded as being only a temporary inhabitant of the body. In some religions the doctrine of rebirth means that the soul is permanently bound to matter, unless release can be attained; even here, however, reality is timeless, in contrast to the unreal world of phenomena, in which time is self-perpetuating. In some religions, the soul may be held to be pre-existent, i.e. by its very nature outside the passage of time, and brought into time only when associated with a mortal body.

The religious world-view also involves distinctive attitudes to time. These are normally taken to be of two kinds: linear and cyclical. In the linear view, found e.g. in Judaism and Christianity, time is a condition of the world as created by God; it has a beginning and will have an end. God is timeless, in the sense that all that we understand as time is within the reality which is God. The cyclical view is similar in its attitude to the present world-order, but it regards this as only one in an unimaginably great series of such worlds. The present order has begun, and will end, but will then be succeeded by a fresh order, similarly doomed to eventual destruction. All religions are, however, to some extent cyclical, i.e. determined by the succession of years, seasons, months (phases of the moon) and days, usually marked by recurrent festivals.

(4, 7, 10, 13, 14, 21, 22, 35, 38)

48 TOTEM: The Ojibwa Indian word "totem" was first used in the West in the late eighteenth century to refer to belief in a "favourite spirit" in animal form among North American Indians. Some tribes, it was recognized, thought themselves to stand, individually and collectively, in a special relationship with certain animals, birds and plants. A group would call itself by the name of the animal in question, and would not normally kill or eat it; it might also be regarded as the ancestor of the group. An individual might also have a "personal totem" or guardian spirit in animal or bird form. It was later noted that the Australian Aborigines had a family and clan structure corresponding in many ways to this North American pattern, and it gradually became usual to locate every instance of the worship of animals under the general concept of "totemism".

The term "totemism" was coined by J. F. M'Lennan in 1869, but not only as a descriptive term; drawing together various instances of the totem phenomenon, and treating them in an evolutionary framework, he formulated "the hypothesis that the ancient nations came through the totem stage". The core of this hypothesis was the assumption that primitive man had first ascribed life and personality to animals, plants and natural objects, and that then a particular tribe had appropriated a special animal or object as the focus of its reverence. Other peculiarities of the system included a custom by which members of a totemistic group might marry only *outside* the group ("exogamy"). The totemistic hypothesis proved popular; it was taken up in various ways by W. Robertson Smith, J. G. Frazer, Emile Durkheim and many other scholars, and is still used by some anthropologists and sociologists.

However, "totemism" as a technical term is potentially misleading. It goes without saying that certain religions have deities which are represented wholly or partially in animal form (the best-known examples being from ancient Egypt and from Hinduism, where the elephant-headed god Ganesha and the monkey-headed Hanuman are popular). It is also undeniable that among some North American Indians and Australian Aborigines there are many totems. But to deduce from this that religion has in all cases passed through a "totemistic stage" is an illegitimate conclusion. Not only does it presuppose a general theory of religious evolution through an artificial series of "stages" (which in fact vary greatly from culture to culture), but it overlooks genuine differences of world-view and social organization. North American and Australian cultures are not identical, and it is a mistake to treat them as merely parts of a hypothetical universal phenomenon.

Totemism may thus be used as a descriptive term, provided that it is carefully defined with respect to its local forms, and that each case is treated strictly on its own merits. As an evolutionary term it has been discarded.

It should be pointed out, finally, that the "totem pole" of the north west of North America is a clan or tribal emblem: as such it is not an object of worship, although it may well include totem symbolism.

(1, 2, 5, 28, 36, 43)

49 **WITCHCRAFT:** The necessary substructure of any belief in witchcraft is a belief in the reality of the spirit-world, and in the supernatural power capable of being controlled by anyone in contact with the spirits. A witch, warlock or wizard is believed to be capable of manipulating supernatural power, either to good or evil ends, and witchcraft is thus closely associated with the practice of magic. Although the word is European, the phenomenon as such is universal. It has considerable affinities with shamanism, particularly in its belief in the spirit-flight and in the operation of spirits generally to cause or cure human ills. To this it should be added that much modern witchcraft is less concerned with the exercise of magical powers than with a refined form of chthonic religion in which fertility rites are important.

The status of witchcraft is determined by the dominant religious orthodoxy of a given time and place. Any religious tradition which regards the lower orders of spiritual beings as actually or potentially evil tends also to regard any concern with them as reprehensible. Hence the repeated characterization of witchcraft as "devil-worship", particularly in periods of intensely orthodox belief. Actually, Satanism (the deliberate worship of a power known to be evil) is a separate and distinct phenomenon in the history of religion.

The comparative study of religion has frequently refused to concern itself with witchcraft, except in so far as there has been a demonstrable connection with the mainstream of religious tradition. However, it is undoubtedly a religious phenomenon, and as such is part of the panorama of religious belief and practice with which the student may legitimately concern himself. Anthropologists, on the other hand, have in recent years been concentrating more and more on witchcraft practices among primitive peoples. More precise distinctions between types of witchcraft have been drawn – for instance, in the relationship between witchcraft and sorcery, "white" and "black" magic, and in the secret societies which involve belief in witchcraft and magic.

It is also worth noting that in a period of declining religious orthodoxy in the West, there has been something of a resurgence of witchcraft. The existence of covens of witches is known in many Western societies; although their beliefs and practices are imperfectly understood, it seems that these have been drawn in many instances from pre-Christian fertility rituals. In the lack of a dominant and intolerant orthodoxy it is unlikely that there will be fresh witch-trials, but on the psychological level, it has been pointed out that the "witch-hunting" mentality still survives in other forms. At all events, the subject as a whole, together with its religious and psychological presuppositions, is one which is eminently worthy of close scholarly study.

(11, 13, 20, 23, 35, 41)

50 WORSHIP is a word used in a very wide sense to denote any action undertaken out of an express desire to honour and serve God or the gods; more specifically it denotes such action as it occurs in a ritual setting. The connection between worship and service is a close one, as can be seen from the etymology of worship: English *divine service*, German *Gottesdienst*, etc.

In the ancient religions it was generally held that man had been placed in the world in order to serve the gods; man's position in the world often paralleled that of the slave in the city-state. Thus it was his duty to care for the gods, to build them homes, to feed them by means of sacrifice, and to ensure their continued benevolence in every way possible. Acts of worship followed daily and seasonal cycles, in accordance with the pattern and rhythm which the gods had themselves established. Whether the deity was actually present (in a cult-image) or symbolically present, worship was entirely directed to him or her. Its elements included thanksgiving for the continued maintenance of the natural order and particular gifts, the singing of hymns of praise, the reading or chanting of prayers, the use of music and dance and seasonal dramatic representation of the great acts of the deity – all bound together by the continual practice of sacrifice.

Worship therefore always acknowledges the inferiority of the worshipper to the being worshipped; it is commonly preceded by acts of purification (ritual washing, confession and absolution); and it very often relies on the good offices of a mediator – shaman, priest, minister – who is peculiarly qualified to approach the divine mystery. Worship is seldom in the history of religion free from restrictions. Non-members of the cultic community would not be permitted to approach or be present at the great acts of corporate worship.

Where the sense of a religious community is strong, worship continues to be of a mainly corporate character; the worship offered in a Jewish synagogue or Christian church is corporate

80

worship, although it is always stressed that individual attitudes are important, and the individual is exhorted to "draw near with faith". In contrast, the Hindu typically views worship as an individual concern, which may be carried out either in the temple or at home. The great festivals assemble great crowds to particular temples or other holy places, but they are crowds of individuals seeking, for the most part, individual merit. Alongside this may be set the American Protestant habit of referring to "worship experience", i.e. to the validity of worship as resting in the mind of the worshipper.

Worship normally follows fixed forms; the Christian term is "liturgy" (Greek *leitourgia*, public service), sometimes restricted to the Eucharist and sometimes used to refer to any Christian ritual. There are, however, freer forms of public worship. Private worship, too, varies very greatly in the strictness of its adherence to prescribed forms, from the daily prayer of the orthodox Muslim and the recitation of the Roman Catholic divine office at one extreme to the Hindu practice of *japa* (continual repetition of the name of God) and free devotional reading at the other. Thus while the forms of worship are easily studied, the meaning of worship to the individual is much less accessible, other than to the psychologist of religion.

(1, 5, 14, 18, 26, 27, 35, 37, 39, 40)

INDEX

The reference is to the number of the article in which the term occurs; frequently occurring references, e.g. to major religions, are not included.

Ahura Mazda 11
Alcheringa 1
anattā 43
Angra Mainyu 11
art 35
asceticism 27, 41
Atharva Veda 9
ātman 43
atonement 37, 42
Australia 1
avatars 19

baptism 4, 20, 26
Bhagavad Gita 37
bhakti 38
Black Mass 23
Bleeker, C. J. 29
blood 4, 39, 42, 45
bodhisattva 38
brahman 27, 30, 43
Brandon, S. G. F. 47
Buddha 19

canon 40
caste 5
celibacy 31
Chantepie de la Saussaye, P. D. 29
Christian Science 40
Christmas 14
Cicero 17, 33
circumcision 20
Codrington, R. H. 24

commitment 32
communion 37
conversion 25
cosmic tree 41
cosmology 7, 16
couvade 4
culture-hero 17

dance 35, 36
Delphi 8
Demeter 26, 38
demiurge 17
Dodona 8
drama 14, 26, 35
Durkheim, E. 5, 6, 33, 48

Easter 14
Egypt 7, 9, 21, 22, 24, 25, 42, 48
eidetic vision 29
Eleusis 13, 26
Eliade, M. 7
Elysian Fields 22
epoché 29
Eskimos 41
ethics 5, 11, 21, 22, 32, 38, 42
Eucharist 26, 37, 50
Euhemeros 17
evolution 2, 6, 10, 15, 24, 29, 48
exogamy 48

family 1, 5, 48
fear 1

fire 37
forgiveness 42
fortune 12
Frazer, J. G. 6, 23, 48

Ganesha 48
ghost 1, 2, 4, 24, 36, 43
Gilgamesh, Epic of 9, 37
Gnosticism 3, 19, 20
Greece 8, 9, 13, 22, 37
guru 5, 40

Hades 22
Hanuman 48
heaven and hell 21, 22
Heiler, F. 30
Hesiod 17
high gods 15, 16
history of religion 33
holy of holies 39
Homer 8
Hume, D. 17
hunters 41

icon 18
idol 18
imām 19
immortality 11
Iran 11, 21
Isis 26, 38

japa 50
Jupiter 13
jyotisa 3

karma 11, 12, 15, 21
khandhas 43
king 18, 19, 22, 30, 31, 34, 36, 39
Krishna 19, 38
84

Lactantius 33
Lang, A. 6, 28
Lapland 41
Lehmann, E. 6
Lévi-Strauss, C. 28
Lévy-Bruhl, L. 6
lingam 18
liturgy 50
Loki 17

ma'at 42
M'Lennan, J. F. 48
Marett, R. R. 24
Marduk 7
marriage 3, 4, 16, 48
mediation 30, 31, 32, 41, 50
Melanesia 24
Menzies, A. 33
Mesopotamia 3, 7, 9, 13, 25, 37,
    38, 42
Mithra 26
monasticism 5, 20
mother-goddess 13, 16
Müller, F. Max 6, 28
music 35

naming 20
necromancy 8
New Year 14
Nirvana 27
Norns 12
North American Indians 17, 20, 48
numinous, the 15

oral tradition 34, 40
ordination 20
origins of religion 2, 6, 15, 36, 47
Orpheus 26, 38
Osiris 21, 26, 38
Otto, R. 15, 36

Palaeolithic religion 4, 18, 22
personality 43
Pettazzoni, R. 12
Plutarch 44
pneuma 43
Polynesia 45
prasada 37
Pratt, J. B. 12, 33
protology 10
pseudo-religions 33
psychology of religion 27, 33, 49
purgatory 21
purification 20, 42, 45

Rama 19, 38
rebirth 11
Rome 13
Ringgren, H. 12, 28
rishi 34
rita 42
rites of transition 4, 20

sacred marriage 13
Samkhya 15
Satan 11, 49
Scandinavia 12, 13, 17, 22
scapegoat 37
Schleiermacher, F. 33
sect 32
Sedna 41
service 50
Sheol 22
Shi'a 19
Shiva 11, 18, 38
shraddha 1
shruti 34, 40
Sikhism 40
Smith, W. R. 48

smriti 40
Snorri Sturluson 17
sociology of religion 5, 33
Söderblom, N. 27, 36
sol invictus 44
sōma-sēma 43
Spencer, H. 1, 17
spirit-possession 19, 32
Stahl, G. E. 2
sun 14, 44
superstition 15
symbol 18, 20, 23, 45, 48

temple 5, 18, 50
theodicy 11
Thor 13, 18
Ti'amat 7
tirtha 37
Torah 40
tradition 31, 32, 34, 40, 44
trance 2
Trickster 17
Tylor, E. B. 2, 6, 9, 24, 28

Valhalla 22
van der Leeuw, G. 29
Varuna 42
Vedangas 3
via negativa 27
Vishnu 19

well-dressing 13
Whitehead, A. N. 33
Widengren, G. 12

Zeus 13, 19
Zoroastrianism 22